Does It Matter
How I Live?

Does It Matter How I Live?

Applying Biblical Beliefs to Your Daily Life

Millard J. Erickson

Study Guides and Teaching Suggestions by Sandra McMaken

8858   10538

Baker Books
A Division of Baker Book House Co
Grand Rapids, Michigan 49516

© 1994 by Millard J. Erickson

First published in 1987 as *Responsive Faith* by Harvest Publications

Published by Baker Books
a division of Baker Book House Company
P.O. Box 6287, Grand Rapids, Michigan 49516-6287

Printed in the United States of America

Library of Congress Cataloging-in Publication Data

Erickson, Millard J.
[Responsive faith]
    Does it matter how I live? : applying biblical beliefs to your daily life/Millard J. Erickson: study guides and teaching suggestions by Sandra McMaken.
    p. cm.
    Originally published: Responsive faith. Arlington Heights, Ill.: Harvest Publications, c1987.
    Includes bibliographical references.
    ISBN 0-8010-3223-7
    1. Christian life—1960—   I. McMaken, Sandra. II. Title.
[BV4501.2.E75   1994]
248.4—dc20   94-5642

To the thirty-six congregations
in which I have served forty-three interim pastorates
from 1964 to the present
This volume is affectionately dedicated

Contents

Preface   9

1. If the Gospel Is So Simple, Why Is Godly Living So Hard?   11
2. When You Absolutely, Positively Have to Know You're Saved   19
3. Getting to Know Your Best Friend Better   31
4. How to Find Success in Your Prayer Life   45
5. Resisting Temptation Without Backing Down   57
6. The Hidden Value of Doubt   69
7. How to Know You Know God's Will   81
8. How to Be Confident You're Doing God's Will   95
9. Giving to God—Many Happy Returns?   107
10. How to Share Your Faith—Without the Butterflies   119
11. God's Cure for Discouraged Hearts   131
12. How to Live on Daily Rations, and Enjoy It   143
13. How to Accept Being Rejected   157

Teaching Suggestions   169

Preface

One of my convictions, stemming from years of interaction with other Christians, is that many of us suffer
from a sense of disparity between what we know and
believe in our Christian lives and how we are actually
living. It is out of this conviction that this book has grown.

I wish to express my appreciation to all who have
helped bring this writing to fruition. Bob Putman edited
the original manuscript and Maria denBoer edited this
revised version, each adding greatly to it by their deft
work. Sandra McMaken's study helps and teaching suggestions have made this book more useful. Typing was
done by Nannette Ward, Kathleen Charles, and Pat Krohn.
Most of all, however, I am indebted to the thirty-six fine
congregations in Illinois, Wisconsin, and Minnesota in
which I have served forty-three interim pastorates since
leaving the full-time pastorate in 1964. The persons in
those churches with whom I have interacted regarding
the ideas in these chapters are too numerous to name.
Those congregations have provided my continuing education in ministry. More than that, they have given me
fellowship, encouragement, and opportunities for deep-
ened understanding of the Christian life. They have taught

me more than I have taught them. Perhaps more accurately, we have learned from the Lord together. It is to those saints of God that this series of studies is dedicated. It is my prayer that all who read these pages may grow in the grace of our Lord Jesus Christ.

1

If the Gospel Is So Simple, Why Is Godly Living So Hard?

Sweating after a long morning of cutting fireplace wood, Tom sat down to eat his lunch. He opened his lunch bucket and pulled out a ham sandwich. Hungrily he bit into it. The sharp taste of dijon mustard bit on his tongue. Then he opened the newspaper that he had brought along and began to page through it.

Suddenly his eyes spotted something that startled him: an advertisement for a chain saw. "Cut up ten trees in one day?" it asked, "With this saw you can." Excitedly, Tom read the entire ad. The manufacturer guaranteed that he would fell and cut up ten average-sized trees in a single day, or the seller would refund the purchase price. *Now this*, Tom thought, *is just what I need*. He burned a lot of wood in his fireplace and the chain saw seemed like the answer to his needs.

Tom hurried to the store and asked about the saw. The salesperson verified that the guarantee stood as advertised. The saw was expensive, but Tom reasoned that it was well worth the price since it would save him time— and time, after all, is money. He bought the saw, resolving to put it to the test the very next day.

Tom worked for the entire next day, but to his disappointment he only cut up two trees. Determined to overcome this deficiency, he rose early the following day and worked harder than before. But at the end of the day he had sawed only four trees.

He concluded that he must be below average in skill. So he got up and began sawing at 6:00 A.M. the next day, working feverishly and almost without interruption until 10:00 P.M. Yet he only cut up six trees, which he calculated to be his maximum output. In disgust he returned the saw to the store where he had bought it and demanded his money back. The salesperson agreed that he would gladly refund the money, but first he wanted to be sure that there was nothing wrong with the saw. He filled the tank with gasoline, flipped the ignition switch to "on," and yanked the starter rope. The engine roared to life. As it did, a startled Tom exclaimed: "What's that noise?"

This story illustrates a point about you and me. As Christians we are like Tom at times. We work hard to live a successful Christian life, but because of our ignorance of God's instructions, our failure to read them, or our inability to understand them, we do not experience his enablement. Instead, we feel disappointed, frustrated, or guilty about our inability to live the Christian life as we believe it should be lived.

Another illustration comes to mind. The writer Thomas Carlyle grew up in a strict Scottish Presbyterian home. One Sunday as he and his mother were walking home from church, he turned to her and said, "If I were the pastor of that church, do you know what I would tell those people, Mother?" His mother, quite surprised at his sudden interest in the ministry, asked, "No, Tommie, what would you tell them?" "I'd tell them," young Thomas said, "'You all know what to do. Now go out and do it!'" His mother, a few years older and wiser in the Christian faith, responded, "Aye, Tommie, and would you tell them *how*?"

Our Tension Between Understanding and Performance

We know a great deal about what we ought to do in our Christian lives, but our knowledge of how to do what we know we ought to do escapes us. We are often frustrated by this tension between our understanding and our performance. We are not unique in this. Even the apostle Paul felt this tension. He gave classic expression to it in Romans 7:18b–19: "I have the desire to do what is good, but I cannot carry it out. For what I do is not the good I want to do; no, the evil that I do not want to do—this I keep on doing."

Much Christian teaching and preaching deals with the "what" of the Christian life—what we ought to believe and what we ought to do. Relatively little teaching is concerned with how the "what" ought to be done. In over thirty years I have preached between 2,500 and 3,000 sermons, some of them more than once. Most of them have been too concerned with what and not enough with how. This is a challenge that all Christian teachers and preachers encounter every time they prepare a lesson or a sermon. Of course, you and I need to notice that the Bible does not depict the Christian life as something done by our own effort. It is not merely our resolve, determination, and effort that bring about the qualities that Paul speaks of in Galatians 5:22: love, joy, peace, patience, kindness, goodness, faithfulness, gentleness and self-control—the "fruit of the Spirit." These are divinely produced qualities, not human accomplishments. When viewed this way, our problem seems somewhat less overwhelming. Paul, in fact, was able to be quite positive when he wrote: "I can do everything through him who gives me strength" (Phil. 4:13).

This is the wonderful promise. For us the Christian life should be one of victory, not defeat; of satisfaction, not frustration. The commands of God are impossible for us to fulfill in our own strength. For instance, Jesus commanded us to love our neighbor as ourselves. Who can do that? What makes his commands possible to fulfill, however, is that he supplies the resources we need to do what he commands. Augustine prayed: "Give what thou commandest and command what thou wilt."

The Germans have a way of putting this, based on a play on words: *Gabe* and *Aufgabe*. *Gabe* is what is given, a gift. *Aufgabe* is what is given up or delivered, a task or an assignment. The two always go together. With one hand God gives us an assignment or task. With the other he gives us the gift or the resource, the grace to fulfill what he wants. One of the underlying principles of this book is that God's grace always is sufficient for believers who really want to fulfill God's expectations for them.

Why This Book Is for You

There are different classes of people whose performance in the Christian life falls short of the teaching of Scripture. Some people do not know what the Bible expects of them. Their problem, at least in part, is ignorance. They probably do not suffer from feelings of guilt. Rather, they simply have a sense of incompleteness or a lack of fulfillment. They need study and instruction in the Christian life, rather than exhortation to do what they ought.

The philosopher Plato thought that all people really needed to be virtuous was to be instructed in the requirements of the moral life. He believed that whoever saw what was right would naturally do it. Although he placed too much emphasis upon the rational or intellectual dimension of life, that does not alter the fact that this ability to know right is very important. It is true here, as in so many other areas, that those who aim at nothing usually hit it. To aim at something, we must know what it is.

Other believers fall short because they know what God says on a subject, but do not really care about fulfilling it. Their problem is indifference. They may not really accept all of the Bible as authoritative, or they may not really have made Christ the Lord of their lives. At least they are not living on that basis currently. These people need to be challenged to recommit their lives to Christ and to accept the divine leadership of the Savior.

A third group who fail in successfully living the Christian life consists of those who know the teaching of the Scripture on a given subject and desire to do it. But they find themselves for some reason unable to achieve that level of performance. This is the struggler, like Paul, whose experience we examined earlier. Strugglers want to resist temptation, to pray effectively, to share Christ's redeeming love with others, but fall short of these ideals. They may know that God has promised to assist them in their performance of these areas of the Christian life, but they do not know how to bring God's resources and promises to bear upon living their lives.

It is especially for this last group that I've written this book: people who are conscientious, concerned Christians like you and me, who honestly want to do God's will, but who do not know how to bring his resources to bear in an appropriate and satisfying fashion. We need instruction on how to utilize God's provisions. We know that God has given us instruction in his Word about what he expects us to be and do. He has also promised his resources and power to enable us to fulfill those commands. And he has told us (or in some cases shown us) how to draw upon his provision. It is on this latter area—divine instruction and example—that I have based the studies in this book. Together we will see, for example, that Jesus commanded his disciples to pray. But he also taught them how to do it.

There does come a limit to the answer to the question, "How?" If I am giving you instructions on how to drive a nail, at some point I will have to tell you to pick up a hammer. If you ask how that is done, I will tell you to place your fingers around the handle of the hammer and flex them. If you ask me how to flex your fingers, I will finally have to say, "Simply flex them." There is no further instruction or explanation that I can give. You simply have to do it. This reminds me of Anne Ortlund's chapter, "How to Sing a Congregational Hymn in One Easy Lesson," in her book *Up with Worship*. The entire chapter consists of one word: "Sing!" Likewise, having read Jesus' instructions on praying, you and I simply need to accept our responsibility and pray.

Thank you for taking the time to read this book. I hope that reading these chapters and applying their teachings will make you a better follower of Christ.

Study Guide

Key Concept Questions

1. How would you answer the question posed by this chapter's title: "If the gospel is so simple, why is godly living so hard?"
2. What does the author identify as a significant deficiency in much Christian teaching and preaching?
3. Describe three different groups of believers whose performance in the Christian life falls short of the standards taught in God's Word.
4. What indispensable resource is available for the believer who really wants to fulfill God's expectation for him or her?

Bible Investigation

The author describes the "struggler" as a person who wants to resist temptation, pray effectively, and share Christ's redeeming love, but who falls short of these ideals. Reflect upon the life of David and consider how he fits this description of a "struggler." Carefully read David's prayer in Psalm 51. What steps can you discover from this passage that we should take in order to bring God's resources and promises to bear upon our lives—especially in the areas of temptation, prayer, and witness?

Personal Life Application

Spend time in meditation and prayer, specifically asking God to guide you regarding those areas in which he would want you to "grow up in your salvation" (1 Pet. 2:2). Record in a notebook for future reference a particularly difficult "struggle" that God has brought to your mind. When you have completed this thirteen-week study, re-read what you have written and note how God has worked in your life in this particular area.

For Further Thought

It appears paradoxical that the successful Christian life cannot be attributed to human effort, yet human effort is necessary for it to be possible. To gain insight into this mystery, read the first and third chapters of Colossians. From these passages identify, first of all, what God accomplishes in the process of spiritual growth. Then identify what the individual believer contributes. In what ways does our relationship to others affect spiritual growth? Do you think it is possible for a person to experience spiritual growth in isolation? Why or why not? (see Gal. 5:16–26).

DOES IT MATTER HOW I LIVE?

2

When You Absolutely, Positively Have to Know You're Saved

1 John 2:1–11

The boy hardened his resolve as they pulled into the church parking lot. *He would not go in.* He would not go through the torture of another evangelistic invitation. No matter what pressure his parents applied, he would not budge from the back seat. He braced himself for the conflict.

To his surprise, after several concerned questions, his parents let him have his way. They neither coaxed nor coerced him to join them. They left him alone to spend the time as he pleased.

It was a warm evening and the church windows were open. The strains of the organ and the rising swell of singing voices carried in the air. The boy listened to the pleading chorus of the hymn "Just as I Am." Painfully, he asked himself again, *Why can't I be saved?*

His parents were members of an evangelical church and had taken him there from infancy. Almost unconsciously he had absorbed the elements of the gospel message: that he, like all human beings, was a sinner. That he could do no human work that would qualify him for God's favor. That God loved him and had given his Son, Jesus Christ, to die as a sacrifice for the boy's sins. That if he believed in Jesus Christ and accepted the grace of God, he would be forgiven and accepted by God.

By the age of nine he had believed all of this and acted upon it—again and again. Whether inadvertently or intentionally some evangelists who had visited his church had conveyed the idea that conversion was always accompanied by a great sense of guilt and remorse for sin. This would result in tears. Then, at the moment of submission to God, these emotions would be precisely reversed. He would be overcome by a sense of forgiveness and restoration, and by a consciousness of God's love for him. Joy would flood his soul and bring virtual ecstasy. His tears of shame and guilt would be changed to tears of happiness. This, he came to understand, was the pattern that was always present—and he had not experienced it.

Nothing was more important to the boy than his relationship to God. He desperately wanted the certainty that he was saved, but apparently God had not accepted him, because he had not experienced this "new birth." He had done everything right. He had taken all the prescribed steps. Yet nothing seemed to happen. Perhaps he had made an error somewhere? He had tried to do it over and over again, to get it right. But still nothing happened. Now, the lyrics of "Just as I Am" sliced at his insides. They were painful, cruel, mocking words. In his imagination, the gaping jaws of hell were opening to greet him. "Why, God, can't I be saved?" he cried.

Days later the boy mustered the courage to ask an older Christian man if he had experienced an emotional conversion. To his surprise, the man said he had not. Then the boy talked to other Christians he respected and found that some of them had felt these strong emotions when they were converted, but others had not. Gradually, he realized the truth that the new birth and its psychological accompaniments were two different things. He had been a Christian for some time, but only now did he find the assurance of it. He resolved that if he ever had the opportunity, he would tell others of his discovery so that they would not have to struggle as he had.

Much to the boy's surprise, God gave him that opportunity. The boy grew up to be a pastor, and later a theology professor and seminary dean. As you've probably guessed, I am the boy in this story.

You Can Be Certain

Many people today can share similar stories about an agonizing struggle with doubt over the certainty of their salvation. For some the struggle is the result of a personal or family crisis that catapults them into questioning. For others it is a battle to produce the right feelings or outward signs in order to be sure that they are "born again." For many, it is a growing uneasiness with their spiritual progress after many years of dedicated faith and service, or the question of why, after being saved, some fall into gross immorality and apparent disbelief.

Whatever the cause, many Christians are tormented by uncertainty about their salvation. As a result, their effectiveness is stunted or inhibited. They participate in the life and work of Christ as far as their comfort level allows, but they are unable to be free. Always, they have that nagging question eating at their confidence: "Are you *really* sure you're saved?"

God does not intend for his children to wander in a wilderness of doubt, frustration, and guilt about the question of their salvation. He has made the issue clear. You either are or are not a Christian, and it will be obvious one way or the other. The book of 1 John was written expressly for this purpose: "that you may know that you have eternal life" (5:13). In this book, John points out the crucial tests of assurance for those who believe in Christ.

An Unchanging Word from an Unchanging God

The first assurance we have is the Word of God. John appeals at several points to the "old command," (2:7) to what his readers have heard (2:18; 3:11). It was apparent that for members of the church the truths received from God were important in shaping and supporting their faith. The Word of God has value in our assurance because of its certainty, clarity, and permanence.

Uncertainty comes from looking at things that are uncertain. You may have read printed pages where the type slipped in the printing process, making a multiple impression. It is confusing and difficult to read. Much uncertainty in the Christian life results from undue reliance upon emotions, which fluctuate as a result of various factors. When the factors change, our feelings are affected as well, and with them our judgment.

A paratrooper was about to make his first jump. The commander told him to jump from the plane, shout "Geronimo," and pull the ripcord, whereupon his parachute would open. If that failed, he was to pull the other ripcord, and the auxiliary chute would open. When he landed on the field below, a truck would be there to bring him back to camp. The man jumped, shouted "Geronimo," pulled the ripcord, and looked up. No parachute appeared. Quickly, he pulled the ripcord for the auxiliary chute, but it didn't open either. In disgust he looked down at the field below and said, "If that isn't just like the Army! I'll bet the truck isn't even there."

In this story, there is no logical connection between the failure of the two parachutes to open and the presence of the truck. What happened, however, was an emotional reaction. The two misfortunes led to the man's feeling, "Everything goes wrong around here." The same thing happens in the Christian life. Some dark, rainy night on your way to an important meeting, wearing your best clothes, you have a flat tire and then discover that your jack is broken. If in that moment you ask yourself, "Am I a Christian?" you may find that you don't especially feel like one. Emotions ride up and down upon the surface of life's experiences. Illness, fatigue, and unfortunate incidents may cause us to lose the feeling of being a Christian, or at least diminish this feeling.

In contrast to this is God's Word. The content of Scripture remains fixed and constant from day to day. Regardless of weather or any other circumstances, we may turn to it and find that it still says the same thing. This is because God himself does not change, nor does his plan. Our salvation rests upon certain accomplished, permanent facts, particularly those connected with the life, death, and resurrection of Jesus. We can find certainty in the biblical record of these facts.

What does the Bible say? Paul announced that "everyone who calls on the name of the Lord will be saved" (Rom. 10:13). Jesus declared, "Whoever hears my word and believes him who sent me has eternal life and will not be condemned; he has crossed over from death to life" (John 5:24). John reported, "Yet to all who received him, to those who believed in his name, he gave the right to become children of God" (1:12). And Jesus promised, "Whoever comes to me I will never drive away" (6:37). The question now is not, "How do you feel?" but rather, "Have you believed and accepted him? Have you sincerely trusted in his grace and asked for his forgiveness?" If we can genuinely answer "yes," then the Scripture is clear: God has saved us, given us new life and made us new creatures.

Your Life Will Be Evidence

John gives us an additional record of the promises and production of God's grace: The Bible is clear on the question of salvation by grace through faith: We are saved by accepting God's gift, not by the accomplishment of our good deeds. It is also abundantly clear that when there is genuine transformation of a life, certain works will inevitably result. These become evidence to us of the reality of the work God has done in our lives. They are not tests we apply to others to determine whether their Christianity is genuine. They are, instead, sources of encouragement to us.

The first of these is *obedience to the commands of Christ.* John says, "We know that we have come to know him if we obey his commands" (1 John 2:3). This is the first question: "Am I keeping the commandments of our Lord?" While we probably will not find our obedience to be perfect, we'll at least see progress and a desire to do even better in this respect. This is evidence of the genuineness of our Christian experience.

As a result, there will be *resemblance to Christ.* John says, "Whoever claims to live in him must walk as Jesus did" (2:6). If we do his commands, we will be like him, for he did the Father's will perfectly. Our increasing conformity to the mind and manner of the Lord is evidence of the genuineness of our personal Christianity.

A third work is *love for the brethren.* John said, "Whoever loves his brother lives in the light, and there is nothing in him to make him stumble" (2:10). He also speaks very strongly to the negative side of this point: "But whoever hates his brother is in the darkness and walks around in the darkness" (2:11). Our love for other Christians involves our desire to be with them, to share the Christian life with them, to give and receive encouragement, instruction, correction, and prayer. More than that, however, love involves active deeds of helpfulness. Love in this biblical sense is not only a warm feeling of liking—and that is good because not all Christians are easy to like (some of them, surprisingly, find us to be the same way). Rather, love is concern for, and active effort to achieve the ultimate welfare of the other person. It includes actions such as laying down one's life for the sake of another person (3:16) and giving material goods (3:17).

The final work of Christian living is *keeping the doctrine of Christ.* In John's day there were people who taught that Jesus was not really human. They said that he was fully God, but he had only taken the appearance of a man. He seemed to be man. John made it clear: "Every spirit that acknowledges that Jesus Christ has come in the flesh is from God, but every spirit that does not acknowledge Jesus is not from God" (4:2–3). Additional belief about Jesus is also important: "Everyone who believes that Jesus is the Christ is born of God" (5:1). According to John, the view we have of Jesus is the clue to our relationship to the Father: "No one who denies the Son has the Father; whoever acknowledges the Son has the Father also" (2:23). Because we accept the full deity and full humanity of Jesus, and honor him as God's Son and as Savior and Lord, we know that we belong to God.

These evidences are encouragements to us. A word of caution is in order, however. Because some Christians are perfectionists, they become excessively aware of the shortcomings in their lives. They see the standard of Christian spiritual maturity and how far short of it they fall, and they become discouraged. They are like people who plant a seed and then keep digging it up to examine its roots. Excessive preoccupation with growth can be as destructive to the life of the spirit as it is to the life of a plant. Rather than probing the discrepancy between what we now are and what we ultimately will be, we ought to note how far we have come from what we once were. If our focus is upon the fact that God is now at work in us, we will allow him to encourage us through what he has done and is presently doing in our lives.

Certainty in the Spirit Within

Finally, we have assurance through the witness of the Spirit. John says, "And this is how we know that he lives in us: We know it by the Spirit he gave us" (3:24). "We know that we live in him and he in us, because he has given us of his Spirit" (4:13). "And it is the Spirit who testifies, because the Spirit is the truth" (5:6). This witnessing effect of the Holy Spirit is an internal activity of God, corresponding to the external work of redemption and of the Scripture.

But what is this witness of the Spirit? Is it a feeling, a subjective impression? If it were simply this, it would suffer from the same defects as our emotions. No, it is deeper than that. It is *conviction*. It is a deep, settled certainty that God creates in our mind and hearts that we are his children. In spite of the perplexity and uncertainties of life, some beliefs become so solid in our minds and hearts that they can be called convictions. They are the very groundwork on which our lives are based.

Jesus spoke of the Spirit bringing to remembrance all that Jesus had said to his followers (John 14:26) and that he would take the things of Jesus and declare these to them (16:14). The Spirit uses various means to accomplish this. Frequently, the Spirit's method of working is to impress upon us the truth and reality of some portion of Scripture. Sometimes as we hear other believers tell what Christ means to them, the Spirit creates a resonance in us, so that we say, "Yes, that's right. I identify with that." At other times, he makes some circumstance reflect the grace that is at work within us.

Several years ago I attended a men's banquet in Chicago. The speakers that night were two Christian young men, Dave Wickersham and Don Demeter, who at the time were players for a major league baseball team. They shared their testimonies of what it meant to be evangelical Christians and major league baseball players. The men and boys present were captivated. During the question time someone asked if it was true that Willie Horton of the Detroit Tigers had become a Christian, and these two men confirmed the report and then told the following story about Willie.

Early in the season Willie was on a hot batting streak. One day he went up to the plate and dug in. The first

DOES IT MATTER WHAT I BELIEVE?

pitch came in, high and inside, straight at his head. Willie dropped to the ground to avoid being hit. He got up, dusted himself off, and dug in again. The second pitch was exactly like the first, and Willie hit the dirt again. He got up, walked to the on-deck circle where Don Demeter was waiting to bat, and said, "Don, now I know I'm a Christian. Last year, if a pitcher had thrown at my head, I would have been out there on the mound working him over with my bat. A new Willie Horton lives in this Detroit Tiger uniform."

I am sure it won't be necessary for you to have baseballs thrown at your head at ninety miles per hour to receive the assurance of your salvation. But whatever means he employs, the Holy Spirit will call to your attention this fact: "You're different from what you once were. You're a child of God." This was the experience of Paul, who said, "I know whom I have believed, and am convinced that he is able to guard what I have entrusted to him for that day" (2 Tim. 1:12).

It is the Lord's intention for us that we not only have his gift of salvation, but also that we know that we have it. If we have doubts, we need to look at the evidence he has provided: the Word of God, the works of the Christian life, and the witness of the Spirit. And then we can go on to enjoy the kind of confident Christian living that he intends for us.

Put It into Practice

To have assurance of your salvation, there are certain steps you can take:

1. Ask yourself sincerely if you have fully placed your trust in Christ for salvation.

2. If your feelings about your salvation seem to fluctuate, ask yourself if there are some other circumstances, including fatigue or illness, which may be contributing to your uncertainty.

3. When doubt about your salvation comes, turn to 1 John and review the instructions and guidelines that John wrote.

4. In evaluating the presence of the works of Christian living in your life, concentrate on how far you have come from where you formerly were, rather than how far you must yet go to where you hope to be.

5. Ask the Holy Spirit to help you recall the experiences through which he has shown you the reality of your salvation in the past.

6. Ask the Holy Spirit to create in you the inward confidence that you have salvation.

Study Guide

Key Concept Questions

1. According to the author, what is the biggest cause of uncertainty in the Christian life?
2. Name three primary sources to which a believer can go for assurance of salvation.
3. What evidences will inevitably accompany a genuinely transformed life?
4. Although it is a worthy goal to strive to live a thoroughly Christian life, what is the danger of an excessive preoccupation with spiritual growth? How should our focus be oriented to avoid this pitfall?

Bible Investigation

Read Romans 8 in its entirety, taking special note of every verse that provides some kind of assurance of salvation. Place each verse in one of the following three categories of assurance: (1) the certainty of salvation found in God's Word; (2) the certainty of salvation as evidenced by a transformed life; or (3) the certainty of salvation as demonstrated by the witness of the Spirit.

Personal Life Application

Suppose a friend of yours was struggling with uncertainty concerning his or her salvation. How would you go about providing the kind of assurance that would enable him or her to go on to enjoy confident Christian living? What specific steps would you suggest that your friend take?

For Further Thought

IDEA A

The author states that the evidences of good deeds that inevitably result from a transformed life are not to be considered tests that can be applied to others to determine whether their Christianity is genuine. Rather, the presence of certain works is a source of encouragement for us. Read 1 John 2:1–11 and 1 John 5:1–5. What ideas do you find in these passages to defend the author's conclusion?

IDEA B

Use the following passages to provide help in describing what is meant by "the witness of the Spirit": John 14:16–17, 25–26; 16:5–15; 1 John 3:24; 4:13. According to these passages, how can the witness of the Spirit be differentiated from feelings or subjective impressions?

3

Getting to Know Your Best Friend Better

John 15:1–17

In the Gospels Jesus uses many images to describe the relationship between himself and his followers. So rich and great is this relationship that no single image suffices to convey it. On one occasion he says, "I am the way" (literally the road). He is the means of access to the Father, the road upon which we travel to get to God. While this picture conveys a significant truth, it is cold and impersonal. There is no real interaction between a road and a traveler.

In the first part of John 15:1–17, Jesus talks about the vine and the branches. This metaphor conveys the idea of vital connection. The spiritual reality of our lives as believers is not generated from within, but comes from Christ, with whom we must be connected. This picture is also rather impersonal. The branches have no consciousness of their connection with the vine, no awareness of the relationship.

Jesus also uses the image of the shepherd and the sheep. While the metaphor suggests some warmth and concern, even conscious interaction, it portrays a relationship of subordination and superordination. The shepherd understands the sheep much more fully than he can communicate with them.

In the latter half of John 15, Jesus develops the highest and most beautiful of images: the believer and Jesus as *friends.* "I no longer call you servants [or slaves]," he says. "I have called you friends" (John 15:15). This picture is one of warmth, closeness, and intimacy.

The Church's Greatest Need

The church of Jesus Christ today has many needs—better preachers, better facilities, more funds. Yet the most important need is for a correct understanding of Jesus Christ and of the relationship believers have with him. We speak a great deal about Christian lifestyle and discipleship. But both of these are strongly influenced by the way we think of Jesus and our relationship to him. One of the greatest problems of the Christian life is to make Jesus real. Somehow he always seems distant or impersonal. We find ourselves trying to relate to a historical figure, but most of the historical personages we know are dead. We do not interact with Julius Caesar, Napoleon, or Martin Luther.

A second problem is that we think of Jesus' teachings and find ourselves related to a set of rules that seem rather cold, formal, and impersonal. Obeying these rules may even be quite mechanical in nature. We think of Jesus as Lord, visualizing him as a lofty, distant tyrant who has no understanding of our situation and no real concern for our needs.

But a friend—someone present, alive, concerned, and understanding—that is different. This was the last impression Jesus gave his disciples. He was soon to be taken from them. It was as if he was saying, "This is how I want you to think of us: as friends." John 15 suggests several characteristics of friendship that are true of our relationship to him.

Friends Are Open and Share

A friendship involves *openness and sharing.* Jesus says, "I no longer call you servants, because a servant does not know his master's business. Instead, I have called you friends, for everything that I learned from my Father I have made known to you" (v. 15). Jesus had shared a great deal with his disciples. He had told them about the Father, the nature of the kingdom, the conditions of fellowship with the Father, his plans for the future. He had explained to them privately the secrets within his parables. They were unable to comprehend or accept some of what Jesus told them. Yet Jesus did not hold back secrets from his friends. The wonders of the kingdom were theirs.

Jesus did not have to tell them these things. He could simply have said, "Believe this. Do this." And they could have responded blindly. Instead of simply telling them what to do, however, he explained the why of it, how it fit into his plans and what it would accomplish. Traditionally, a master or employer often did not share reasons or plans with employees. It was not their place to ask "Why?" in response to an instruction. They did not need to know why; they needed to carry out the orders. Today's participative management techniques are partially changing this situation. Perhaps they are more in line with Jesus' example.

Jesus' friendship for us is demonstrated in what he has revealed. We not only have what the disciples had—the Old Testament and Jesus' teachings. We also have the interpretation and application of these things in the New Testament letters, and the record of how the Holy Spirit worked in the lives of the believers in the early church (Acts). There is room for growth in our understanding, always a challenge for further study and development. What Christian so fully understands the Bible that there is nothing new to learn? What Christian can answer all the questions about the Book of Revelation?

If Jesus has so opened himself to us, entrusting every secret of the kingdom to us, then we can be open with him. We need not be secretive about our innermost needs, concerns, hopes, and fears. With our best friend we can share anything.

Jesus knows all about us. What we hide from others, and even from ourselves, is completely transparent to him. In theory, of course, we know that he already knows what we will say before we tell him. In view of this, we might be inclined to think it does not matter whether we share these things with him. Yet it is quite another thing to acknowledge our secrets to him, so that we can deal with them openly.

Jesus knows us fully, and that provides a wonderfully liberating experience. We do not have to pretend or put on our best behavior for him. We can be completely honest; we can be ourselves with him. We can discuss and confess and pray about the most intimate and embarrassing matters, realizing that he knows, understands, and does not condemn us. This is how friends are. We can be ourselves. We do not have to put on a good front or try to make a good impression. We can relax.

Several years ago when I was teaching in a Christian liberal arts college, I came into the department office one day. The department secretary, whose husband taught in the history department, said to me, "Some of us have been feeling sort of depressed. We thought we'd get together, have a potluck supper and just let our hair down. Would you like to come?" It was the end of February, the psychological low point of the school year, at least in the northern part of our country. So we went. A variety of people were there: a physics professor, one each from economics, history, archaeology, and other departments. There were no two people from the same department. Everyone there was an assistant professor; there were no associate professors or full professors, no administrators. No one who would ever have to make an official evaluation of anyone else present, so far as we knew. We did not have to maintain our professorial decorum. We were free to be ourselves. It was one of the most enjoyable experiences I have ever had. Likewise, Jesus has taken us into his confidence and we can do the same with him, because we are friends.

A Friendship That Bestows Love

Friendship is also *characterized by love.* Read John 15 carefully and count the number of occurrences of the word "love," either in verb or noun form. (The word appears nine times in the passage, eight of those between verses 9 and 13.) Obviously, Jesus attached considerable importance to this idea. The love that is here placed at the very center of the relationship is not the kind of love that we often hear about in human relationships. Rather, this is the unselfish love that does not seek other people for what we can *get from* them but for what we can *do for* them. This love bestows value rather than extracts it. It does not love because of the quality and value that it finds there, but simply because of what it can do for the person who is the object of that love.

This friend is interested in us for our welfare, that our "joy may be complete" (v. 11). Sometimes an employer is interested in the employee only for the sake of his or her usefulness. During one summer of my student years I worked in a sheet metal factory on Chicago's south side. It was a real sweatshop. I was running a grinder, grinding down ridges left by the welder. One morning I looked into the mirror and saw a small speck in the iris of my right eye: a particle of steel from the grinder had somehow gotten past my protective goggles and embedded itself in my cornea. I was sent to the company doctor, who removed the particle. But it had been there so long that it had rusted, and now I had to be sent to an ophthalmologist to have the rust removed. Almost as if he thought I had incurred the injury intentionally, the foreman reprimanded me: "You have to be more careful. If we keep having these accidents our insurance premium will go up." In that moment I could not have cared less about the insurance premium, or the company. It was apparent that this man had no interest in me as a person, only as a useful worker. With Jesus, it is not so.

Jesus' love is a persistent love. Because it loves for the sake of the other, this love does not drop away simply because of something disagreeable another person does, or something unfavorable we discover about that person. A friend is someone who knows all about you—your good points and your bad—and is still your friend. This is how Jesus has loved us. He does not cast us off because we fail him, or because we sin. Jesus' love for Peter did not end when Peter denied him. His kind of love forgives—not just seven times, but as many as seventy-seven times (Matt. 18:21–22). It forgives and keeps forgiving. We need not be insecure around such love, because it will not easily be lost.

There is a reverse side to this sort of love. When we realize the way in which our friend Jesus loves us, we are moved to love him in that same way. We will love him not merely for what we obtain from him, for what he does for us, but for what we can do for him. If we want him simply for the favors he does for us, we may *have* more because of him, but we will not necessarily *be* better persons. We will actually become more selfish and self-centered. If, on the other hand, we love him simply out of a desire to serve and please him, we will change. We will be reinforcing the tendencies toward unselfishness and altruism. There is a poem that puts this matter of friendship quite well. The first line illustrates the point that we are considering here: "I love you not only for what you are, but for what I am when I am with you." If we have experienced the unselfish, unqualified love of Jesus and if we

DOES IT MATTER HOW I LIVE?

are loving him in that same way in return, we will be becoming the type of person that he is.

When we love for what we get from a relationship, we tend to be disappointed. Our love cools when the person fails to live up to our expectations. I spoke earlier of Jesus forgiving us because we are his friends. I am going to say something that may sound a bit blasphemous at first. If you bear with me, I think you will find that it is not. It is simply this: If we have this type of friendship—love for the Lord—it will enable us to forgive him as well.

Life does not always bring the experiences we want, or which we think ought to take place. Sometimes we cannot understand why some things happen. We pray, and we do not receive answers. We wonder what Jesus is doing, why he is not treating us better. And we may start to feel resentful. In our ordinary human friendships, expectations are sometimes disappointed. Suppose a friend goes away, promising to write every day. The first day goes by with no mail, and then a second, and a third day, and a week. By the middle of the second week we begin to wonder if the postal service is still in operation. What do we do then? This is the test of our relationship. If we have a shallow kind of love, we might simply say, "If that's the kind of friend that she is, we're through as friends—I won't be her friend any longer." But if there is real depth to our love, if it is true love, we say, "I don't know why my friend hasn't written, but I know that there must be a good reason." True love "understands," even when it doesn't understand. It empathizes, even when it doesn't comprehend. And it therefore "forgives." Times come when we do not understand what Jesus is doing, or why, but if we have true love for Jesus, we will not turn away from him. We will continue to love him and trust him nonetheless.

Obeying Is a Love Response

Friendship is *characterized by obedience.* Jesus says, "You are my friends if you do what I command" (John

15:14). The same idea is found in John 14:15, 21, 23. Jesus firmly rejects two opposing erroneous approaches. The first is "slavishness"—the approach that says, "I have to do this, because if I do, my master will reward me." Or worse: "I must do this, because if I do not, my master will punish me." This is how servants or slaves think about their relationship to their masters. A present-day term for this approach is legalism.

The second viewpoint could be called indifference or liberatarianism. It is the view of the liberated former slave. This philosophy is, "I am under grace, I am not required to do this, so I won't." Note that as different as these two philosophies appear on the surface, they rest upon basically the same central principle: "I do only what I have to." The former says, "I have to do this, so I do it." The latter says, "I don't have to do this, so I don't."

Jesus steers a middle course between these two erroneous extremes. He does not say, "You are under grace, not under the law, so you can do as you please." Nor does he say, "You had better do what I tell you, because our relationship depends upon it." Rather, he says, "We are friends, and these are the requests that I have of you. It would please me very much if you did these things." Notice that this motivation is not coercive, but appeals to the warmth and quality of our relationship to him.

If we are seeking to please our Lord, we will search the Scriptures to find the commands that he has given—and there are plenty to find. We will not simply feel warm, positive feelings toward him. He has given us specific commands to carry out. It is not legalism to have definite patterns and requirements that we carry out. No, legalism is the spirit of doing something *because* it is a rule, not the fact that we follow specific rules.

When I was a boy, ice cream was a real luxury in our home. We did not have a refrigerator, only an old-fashioned icebox, and ice cream would not keep in it. When

DOES IT MATTER HOW I LIVE?

we brought home a pint of ice cream, we had to eat it immediately. There were three of us kids, in addition to our parents. As you'd expect, disputes developed over who received the largest portion. On one occasion I laid a ruler alongside the brick of ice cream, calculated exactly one-fifth of the length to the millimeter (I was good at mathematics), marked these measurements on each edge, top and bottom and each side, and cut the ice cream into five exactly equal portions. That was legalism.

It is not legalism to say that each person should receive an equal amount; that is simply "lawism," or perhaps better stated, "fairness." But to measure exactly, as I did, so that the letter of the rule is painstakingly kept—that is legalism. It is not legalism to tithe because you believe that the Lord has commanded us to give one-tenth of our income to him. But I once knew a man who carried a small notebook with him everywhere he went. On one side of the page he recorded every cent of income he received, and on the other side every cent he gave to the Lord. At the end of the year he made certain he had given precisely, to the nearest cent, one-tenth of all he had received. To give exactly one-tenth, no more and no less, and in effect to say to the Lord, "I have done what you asked of me, and you cannot ask anything more whatsoever"—that is legalism! If we have understood Jesus' approach to obedience, we will not ask, "What *must* I do?" but rather, "What *may* I do?"

A man who was my friend since our college days recently passed away. He had a car during college and I did not, and when he went away on vacation he left it with me for safekeeping and to use. When he was doing research for a master's thesis in plant genetics, I spent hours at night helping him wash his radioactive corn. Over the years since college, we each moved from place to place, maintaining contact and remaining as friends. For the last several years of his life, my friend Dave lived in Phoenix. He was legally blind.

Periodically, he would travel to Chicago for seminars. On one of those occasions, I asked if he had any time free to come to our home for dinner. He checked his schedule and indicated that Tuesday night was free. I drove from our home in Wheaton to pick him up at his motel room near O'Hare Field—forty-five minutes of very difficult driving in heavy traffic. I drove him to our house, we had dinner for about two hours, then I made another round trip to O'Hare—a total of three hours of difficult driving, on the night before a day on which I had four classes.

You might say, "It is terrible that your friend demanded that of you!" But you see, he never even suggested it. I knew what it is like to be alone, away from your family in a strange city for several days, and I was sure it must be much worse when you are blind. I knew it would please Dave and make him happy and that's why I did all the driving, that and the fact that it pleased me to see him. Before Dave left the car that night, he invited me and my family to spend that Christmas with him and his family in Phoenix. Why did he do that? Because he felt obligated to return my favor? No. He did it simply because that's the kind of thing that friends do for each other.

To see that Jesus says to us, "My friend, these are the things that I need done, and it would please me so if you would do them" will transform our attitude and our actions.

Jesus is a real person, a real friend. A former student wrote of her experience on an examination I once gave. She had been dating a young man, but knew that the relationship was wrong. She knew she should break it off, but could not do so. Then she went away on vacation for two weeks. When she returned she felt nothing for him. She wrote, "What had happened was that for the first time in my life Jesus had become a real person, capable of fulfilling needs in my life." Was she saying that she had transferred her romantic love to Jesus? No, she had found that Jesus was a friend, in a time when she needed a friend to rely upon.

Christianity is unique among the world's religions. It holds to belief in an all-powerful God who has created all that is and is in control of it. But there are other religions that hold that view. What makes Christianity different from any other religion is that this almighty God has stepped down from heaven, and without ceasing to be God, has become human. And that person reaches out his hand to us and says, "Hello, I'm Jesus. I want to be your friend."

Put It into Practice

To make Jesus a real person who is part of your life you can:

1. Read the teachings of Jesus and notice how open and free he was with his followers. Notice especially the difference between his talks with his friends and his public addresses to crowds. Study the other portions of the Bible, such as the letters of Paul and the Book of Revelation, to notice what amazing mysteries he shared.

2. Notice the passages that teach that Jesus knew the hearts of people, such as in Luke 9:47. Remember that he knows all about you, even your thoughts. Since he knows all of this, you will never surprise or shock him by what you tell him. You are only agreeing with what he already knows about you.

3. Study the way in which Jesus dealt with people who failed him or did not live up to his expectations—Peter, Thomas, James, and John, and recognize that the continuing friendship between him and you does not require you to keep his commands perfectly.

4. Ask yourself what you might do that would bring happiness to the heart of your friend, Jesus. Observe the commands he gives, and try to think of them not as demands that he would enforce but as requests that would bring him joy.

In reading the Bible, picture Jesus actually speaking or writing the words to you in person.

DOES IT MATTER HOW I LIVE?

Study Guide

Key Concept Questions

1. What does the author feel is the most important need in the church today? What are two problems associated with fulfilling this need? How did Jesus define his relationship to his followers in order to satisfy this most important need?
2. Name three characteristics of the unique friendship that believers share with their Lord.
3. Our friendship relationship with Jesus is to be characterized by obedience, but often the way we approach obedience is incorrect. Describe two erroneous extremes relating to the motivation people have for doing what Jesus commands them to do.

Bible Investigation

In Scripture, special mention is made of the unique friendship shared between David and Jonathan. Read the story of their friendship in 1 Samuel 18:1–4; 19–20; 23:16–18; 2 Samuel 1. What elements of this friendship can be likened to that Jesus extended to his followers?

Personal Life Application

Read John 15:9–17. Consider the ways in which a believer actually lives out a friendship relationship with Jesus. Notice the emphasis Jesus makes on the element of love. Read 1 Corinthians 13 in order to more fully understand the way believers are to reflect God's love in their relationships with each other.

For Further Thought

Scripture teaches that to become a "friend of the world" is to jeopardize our friendship with Jesus (James 4:4). How does this teaching reconcile with Jesus' command to "love your neighbor as yourself" and "go make disciples of all nations"? Read Matthew 15:2; 1 Corinthians 5:9–13;

2 Corinthians 6:14–18; 7:1; and James 4:1–10, and to help you with your answer. Does the reverse of James' assertion also hold true? That is, if we choose to be friends of God, does that make us enemies of the world? Why or why not? (See John 15:18–25).

DOES IT MATTER HOW I LIVE?

4

How to Find Success in Your Prayer Life

Luke 11:1–11

Judy was looking forward to her first golf lesson. For some time she had wanted to begin playing golf, but a friend had cautioned her to take lessons before beginning to play. "You'll get off to the right start that way," her friend had advised. Now the time had come, and she showed up for the first lesson, a borrowed five iron in hand. There were lots of practice booths in the classroom, where beginners could hit golf balls into nets. When the instructor appeared, she asked each student to take one of the practice areas. *At last,* thought Judy, *I will get to hit a ball.* But first the instructor taught them how to stand. *Stand?* thought Judy. *I have been standing for years.* The instructor's next subject was grip. Only after these fundamentals were mastered did the instructor allow her to swing a club.

Kevin's first experience with piano lessons was similar. Although he was only in second grade, he was excited about playing songs on the piano so he could enjoy whatever music he wanted to, whenever he wanted. He wondered what song he would learn to play first. But before that could happen, the teacher had him practice holding his fingers the proper way, and then practice scales over and over again. Like Judy, he learned that there are certain basics, certain fundamentals, which must be learned before a skill can be successfully mastered.

The Christian life is like this. One of the basics of the Christian life is prayer. Without proper understanding and skill in prayer, other parts of the Christian life are often ineffective. Perhaps you feel frustrated about your prayers and wonder if they are accomplishing anything.

Probably it was this realization that led the disciples to ask Jesus to teach them to pray. They had seen him praying and desired to be able to pray as he did. They realized that the relationship which he had with his Father was fundamental to everything he did, and they wanted to learn from someone who obviously knew how to pray. "Lord, teach us to pray," they asked simply. Jesus' answer to them applies to us as well, since we have the same needs. His answer to their request included several elements. From his own prayer life the disciples had seen the need for, frequency of, and duration of prayer. Jesus then gave them a model prayer, showing them what to pray about. He also told them a parable, showing them how they were to pray. Finally, he taught them something about the nature of the Father, as an encouragement to prayer. We will focus primarily upon the parable in this chapter.

In the parable of the guest, Jesus emphasized petitionary prayer. He made clear in "the Lord's Prayer" that prayer includes other elements such as praise and confession. In this parable, however, the focus is especially upon the request that we bring to God, asking him to do something or supply something. Prayer can be and will be effective, said Jesus, if we meet certain basic conditions or requirements.

Successful Prayer Emerges from Need

The first requirement for successful prayer is to have a need. The story Jesus told his disciples involved a man who was in bed. It was midnight. Then, unexpectedly, a friend arrived from a journey, weary and hungry. The first man, being a good friend, also wanted to be a good host. But he had no food in the house to feed his visitor. What would he do?

While this story is a bit removed from our twentieth-century experience, it would not be strange for a Jew of Jesus' time. Communication was virtually nonexistent, so that guests often arrived unannounced. Nor is it peculiar that the visitor came at midnight. Anyone who has traveled in Palestine knows that certain parts of it have a desert type of geography. Today, when we find it necessary to travel across a desert, we often delay our trip until after the sun has set, or rise and travel in the very early morning hours. The Palestinian traveler of Jesus' day sometimes traveled by night. That is why this guest came at an awkward hour.

The problem was a difficult one for the host. He wanted to feed his guest, but he had nothing available in the house. There was no merchant to buy food from at this hour of night. He had no solution to the problem, other than seeking out a friend who might lend him what he needed. His need was genuine and serious—the need for food. While some needs might be optional (such as cool water for washing the man's feet, for example), this one was urgent. And his need was an unselfish one. He did not seek food to supply his own desires. It was for someone else.

In this parable Jesus is saying to us that the kind of prayer that is effective is prayer that stems from genuine need. We need a certain amount of boldness to go to God with requests, and boldness is more likely and more properly present when genuine need exists. God is more likely to grant requests for what we genuinely need rather than what we simply desire.

Some of our requests are not really needs. They are simply wants. A poll of Americans taken recently asked them what they considered necessary in life. Many of the items they named did not even exist one hundred years ago. They were not necessities. Our wants have a way of expanding and of seeming to be essential. God has not promised to supply everything we want. He has, however, promised to supply all our needs (Phil. 4:19). James says that his readers ask and do not receive because they ask selfishly to gratify their own desires (4:3).

We need to ask ourselves what our *real* needs are. What is the minimum that will meet those needs? That's what we pray for. God is a generous God, and he generally supplies more than we ask for, more than we absolutely need. Some Christians consider it a mark of great faith to pray for luxurious provisions, on the theory that "God wants the best for his followers" and that "children of the king ought to travel first-class." That God may desire to provide generously for our needs is one thing; that we should expect and require it is another. I may genuinely need an automobile to do God's work. I can therefore pray confidently that God will provide it. But I would have difficulty praying for a BMW or a Mercedes Benz if a less luxurious vehicle would suit the purpose equally well. In Jesus' parable, the man's request was for necessities, not for luxuries. Our prayers will be effective if our requests are for genuine needs.

We may have to develop a sense of concern and burden for some of the genuine needs that exist in our world. Those who have never heard the message of salvation in Jesus Christ need to hear the gospel. People who are suffering, even dying, because they lack the essentials of life maintenance need to have those essentials provided. If we do not feel the weight of these needs we will probably not pray much for them. We can acquire concern for these kinds of needs by reading God's Word, which speaks quite explicitly and emphatically about these matters; by exposing ourselves to the conditions of these people; and by praying that God will make us aware of these needs and cause us to feel them. Real need is essential to effective prayer.

Successful Prayer Is Built on Friendship

A second essential of effective prayer is to have a friend. When the man in Jesus' parable needed to turn to someone for help, he could not go to just anyone. His request was an inconvenient one, even unreasonable. Strangers and even many friends would have turned him away. His friend may have been the only person to whom he could confidently go in a situation like this, because they had an established relationship upon which he could draw.

To bring this a little closer to our experience, imagine that your car stalls in your hometown at two o'clock in the morning. You need help, but you do not belong to an auto club and no towing companies are open. You do not have money for a cab. At the very least, you need a ride home. Your only hope is to call a friend (let's for the moment forget about any relatives). Whom would you call? This is a real test of whom you consider to be your friends, isn't it? There are some people you might put on your list, but if you called them your list of friends would be shorter than it was before. In a situation like this, you would not dare to call a stranger. It would be a waste of time and money.

A doctor in a Minnesota village received a telephone call in the middle of the night from a patient who also was his friend. The man's mouth was bleeding. The doctor, seeking to determine the nature of the problem, asked his friend whether or not he had sustained any wound or injury. The caller indicated that he had had a tooth extracted earlier in the day. "Then why didn't you call the dentist?" The doctor inquired. "What?" replied the friend. "At an hour like this?"

Our relationship to God will determine the effectiveness of our prayer because it will determine whether we will dare come to him with our requests. It also will determine what types of things we will expect him to want to do. If we have neglected our relationship to him, if we have not been praying regularly, reading our Bible, worshiping him seriously, or obeying his commands, we may well feel the way we would about calling a stranger or a neglected friend about our problem at 2:00 A.M. At the least, we must take some preliminary steps to renew the friendship before we bring our requests to him.

If, on the other hand, we have maintained a strong and warm relationship, things will be quite different. We will then know that we can bring our concerns to him and that he is not too busy to be bothered. We'll know he won't be irritated by our asking, but that he is willing and even eager to answer our prayer. We will be bold in coming to him, not timid. And we will know from experience what types of things he desires to do, so that we will know what requests to bring to him.

Make sure that you are maintaining a friendship relationship to God. Your prayer life should be regular rather than sporadic. With some people, regular contact does not foster a friendship; rather, it produces irritation. Because God is always loving, gracious, and dependable, we will find that the love within our relationship with him grows with continued contact.

Successful Prayer Is Persistent

A third essential requirement for successful prayer is to have persistence. The friend who knocked on the door did not meet with immediate success. The friend in the house was in bed with his children. To rise and open the door would probably have disturbed all of them. He was scarcely willing to risk this. So he asked the friend outside

DOES IT MATTER HOW I LIVE?

to go away and not disturb him and his family. The man in need was not easily deterred from his purpose, however. He continued to knock and to ask. The man inside then got up and gave him what he wanted. Jesus' comment on this situation was, "I tell you, though he will not get up and give him the bread because he is his friend, yet because of the man's boldness he will get up and give him as much as he needs."

What Jesus taught in this parable, he then underscored in a direct comment: "So I say to you: Ask and it will be given to you; seek and you will find; knock and the door will be opened to you. For everyone who asks receives; he who seeks finds; and to him who knocks, the door will be opened" (Luke 11:9–10). The full meaning of these two verses is concealed by the English translation. In Greek the verb tense emphasizes continuing action. Thus, a literal translation of these verses would be, "Continue to ask, and it will be given you; persist in seeking, and you will find; keep on knocking, and it will be opened to you. For everyone who continues to ask receives, and he who persists in seeking finds, and to him who keeps on knocking it will be opened." It is continuing, persistent prayer that brings results.

But what are we to make of this teaching? Is God a reluctant Father who only grudgingly gives to insistent children something that he does not really want to give and would not otherwise bestow? That hardly seems consistent with the picture of God that we find elsewhere in Scripture, such as "no good thing does he withhold from those whose walk is blameless" (Ps. 84:11). Why then do we need to be persistent?

Prayer is not changing the mind of God. It is allying ourselves with his purposes, rather than enlisting him for ours. Prayer consists of demonstrating to God that we really do desire what we say we do. It does not take much concern and conviction to pray about a matter once and then forget about it. But to pray about something repeatedly, fervently, requires a genuine concern that approaches that of God himself. While some Christians think it spiritual to pray about something once and then "leave it with the Lord," this teaching of Jesus suggests otherwise. Continuing to pray about a matter is not lack of faith in God's willingness to do what we ask and to supply what we need. Rather it demonstrates the seriousness of our concern.

The president of a college where I formerly taught once told his faculty about the president of a college where he had previously been dean. The man would uniformly deny any request made of him. If the same request were made a second time, or seven more if necessary, he would frequently grant it. When asked why he would later give something he had previously denied, he replied, "If a person doesn't believe in something strongly enough to ask more than once, it isn't worth granting. But if he is really sold on an idea enough to keep on asking despite denials, then he will do something with it when it is given." I was a department chairman and shortly after that time I had occasion to request something for the department from the president. His reply came back, "Request denied." On the theory that this man approved the practice of the man whom he had described, I waited a week or two, then sent the same request, somewhat differently worded, to the president's office. This time the reply came down, "Request granted." Persistence is often rewarded.

Prayer pays. But Jesus wanted to give one additional assurance: that our prayers will be answered in the right way: "Which of you fathers, if your son asks for a fish, will give him a snake instead? Or if he asks for an egg, will give him a scorpion? If you then, though you are evil, know how to give good gifts to your children, how much more will your Father in heaven give the Holy Spirit to those who ask him!" (Luke 11:11–13). God will not disappoint us by giving evil when we ask for good.

DOES IT MATTER HOW I LIVE?

By itself, this seems rather obvious. I think there may be something more here. Sometimes the child seeing a snake thinks it is a fish, and asks for it. Sometimes a child mistakes a scorpion for an egg and says, "Daddy, give me that egg." But the father, being much wiser, does not grant what the child asks for. God, in his infinite wisdom, love, and goodness, at times has to protect us from our own requests. We need not fear that our requests are imperfect; he sees to it that we receive what is good.

Jesus said this is how to pray effectively: have a need, have a friend, and have persistence. And then simply trust a good and wise and loving Father.

Put It into Practice

To insure that your prayers will be effective, you should:

1. Make sure that you keep your relationship with God warm and active. That means that you regularly pray, worship, and study the Bible whether or not you feel like it. Tell him of your love and gratitude, and confess sins that introduce barriers between you and him. Seek by his help to obey his commandments.

2. Carefully scrutinize your prayers and your motives for praying them, to make certain that you are not merely asking to satisfy your own wants or desires, rather than to fulfill genuine needs.

3. Study God's Word and expose yourself to the needs of his world, to discover the real needs and to determine what God is most desirous of doing. Concentrate on praying what God would want you to pray, rather than what you would most want.

4. Pray persistently. Do not merely repeat a prayer in rote fashion, but continue praying regularly, believing that God will answer. Pray with a spirit of not imposing your will upon God, but of demonstrating to him how

important this matter is to you, and how sincere your desire to see it come to pass is.

5. Have confidence that God, as a good God, will not allow any foolish prayer to come to pass, but will give you what is ultimately best for you and all others who are involved.

Study Guide

Key Concept Questions

1. Describe the three basic conditions or requirements that must be met before prayer can be effective.
2. Why are believers encouraged to concentrate on praying for genuine needs rather than "wants"?
3. What do *we* gain in our prayer life by tuning in and praying for the needs of suffering people?
4. What neglected areas in our relationship with God can adversely affect our prayer life?
5. Why can't we just pray about a matter once and then forget about it, "leaving it with the Lord"?

Bible Investigation

Read through the Lord's Prayer in Luke 11:2–4 and then the prayer of Nehemiah in Nehemiah 1. How does Nehemiah's prayer follow the model that Jesus provided for his disciples? What specifically was Nehemiah asking God to do? Was Nehemiah being presumptuous in asking God to do such a specific thing? Why or why not? In what ways did Nehemiah meet the conditions for effective prayer discussed in this chapter?

Personal Life Application

Have you ever felt as if your prayers were "bouncing right back off the ceiling"? Perhaps when this happens we need to remind ourselves of what it is that prayer is intended to accomplish. The author reminds us that prayer is not changing the mind of God. It is allying ourselves with God's purposes, rather than enlisting him for ours. Perhaps we need to regularly evaluate our prayer life in light of this understanding. Scripture demonstrates that to ally oneself with God's purposes is a process that really goes beyond those moments we actually spend on our knees having a conversation with God. Read James 4:1–10. From this passage discover what else is involved in allying ourselves with God's purposes. List some reasons why your own prayer life may not always be as effective as it could be.

For Further Thought

IDEA A

Skim through the story of Asa, king of Judah, found in 2 Chronicles 14–16. Note the differences in the way Asa responded to three different crises in his life: the battle with the Cushites (14:8–15); the military threat posed by Baasha, king of Israel (16:1–6); and the affliction with severe disease in his feet (16:12–13). What can we learn about the role of prayer in each of these situations? What made Asa's prayer in the first instance so powerful? (see 2 Chron. 14:2–7).

IDEA B

Use the understandings about prayer presented in this chapter to form a response to well-intentioned people who draw the conclusion from such passages as Mark 11:22–24 that believers should use prayer to "name it and claim it." (It will be very helpful to pay close attention to the context from which the Mark passage is taken).

5

Resisting Temptation Without Backing Down

Matthew 4:1–11

For Jim, it was one time too many. He needed to get to church a few minutes early to set up the room for the Sunday school class that he was teaching. His immediate obstacle was his wife, Rhonda. He had reminded her the night before that he needed to be there early, but a few minutes after breakfast she sat down to read the Sunday newspaper, and now she was not ready to go. "Why do you do this to me?" Jim blew up. He did not swear, but he might as well have. He told Rhonda what he thought of her. Everything he said was true, but later he realized he had given in to his most common temptation: loss of temper.

Denise knew that the test tomorrow would be an important one, and the material was difficult. Her mother asked her if she shouldn't be studying. Denise, however, was not concerned. She was sure she'd be able to get a C on the test based on what she had learned in class. And whatever she got on this test, she'd pass the course. Her temptation here, as in so many other parts of her life, was to be lazy.

"There's nothing certain in life except death and taxes." So states one of the adages of our culture. For the Christian something else is sure: temptation. To be alive, to be a Christian, is to experience temptation, for the devil is alive, well, and active. His whole purpose of being is to oppose Christ and his followers. If we are unaware of his temptations, then either we are not sensitive enough to sin to recognize them, or we are not vital enough Christians to be very important targets for his attacks.

Though temptation is inevitable, sin is not. From a relative disbelief or disregard of Satan a few years ago, our society and the church now focus perhaps too much attention on Satan. "If Satan is active in this world and is more powerful than I," goes one line of thinking, "how can I resist? I sinned, but I just couldn't help myself." The thrust of Matthew 4:1–11 and the rest of Scripture is that we need never say, "The devil made me do it." Although his efforts at temptation are strong, they are never irresistible for the Christian who is drawing upon the resources God has provided. Our example, Jesus Christ, and his experience of temptation give us guidance on how to do this. Like Christ, we can successfully resist temptation if we correctly understand the factors at work in temptation and act upon that knowledge.

Know Your Weak Spots

We must first know ourselves. The ancient Greeks made this their dictum because they believed that truth lay within the individual. In facing temptation, we must have self-knowledge for virtually the opposite reason. We must know our points of potential vulnerability so that we will be especially alert to the dangers.

Jesus once fasted for forty days and forty nights. Matthew says, "Afterward he was hungry." Jesus was genuinely human as well as completely God. Indeed he was in a sense more human than you or I, because he was what human being was before the fall spoiled human nature.

DOES IT MATTER HOW I LIVE?

When he went without food his body felt the pangs of hunger as genuinely as would yours or mine. Jesus was aware that he wanted food and that consequently he would not react reasonably to the issue of whether or not to eat. He understood that he was especially susceptible to suggestions to eat and that temptation was likely to come at that precise point. And it did. Jesus resisted the devil's suggestion because he was prepared to be attacked at a weak spot.

We need to know ourselves well enough to know our strengths and weaknesses. We are naturally more resistant to some types of temptations and more susceptible to others, simply by virtue of the type of people that we are. Some of us have relatively little problem with laziness, but must be constantly on guard against impatience. For others it is just the opposite. Whether you call it temperament or conditioning, there are real differences among us. Further, our circumstances vary so that what is at one time no problem may at another time be a very serious danger. We need to be aware that our strengths and weaknesses may shift in new situations.

James pointed out that temptation arises because there are things within us that can be targets for temptation. He wrote: "But each one is tempted when, by his own evil desire, he is dragged away and enticed" (1:14). Sometimes the appeal of temptation is to desires that in themselves are natural and good, but may be expressed inappropriately. There is nothing inherently sinful about eating. God gave us the hunger drive to keep us alive. When Satan tempted Jesus to turn stones into bread, he was not appealing to a sinful tendency in Jesus. Rather he suggested an inappropriate or improper fulfillment of a natural function. At other times, however, our own sinful tendencies such as self-centeredness become the target of temptations. Self-understanding consequently is very important.

This means that we must resist the first suggestion of temptation. Sometimes we are approached to make a purchase, or see something in a window or showroom that we want, but we know we should not buy it. But it is pleasurable to look at the object, hear it described, or try it out, even though we know we will not buy it. Then, before we realize it, out comes the credit card and we have made the purchase. Similarly, sometimes the suggestion of a sinful act comes to mind. We of course have no intention of committing the act, but we find thinking about it pleasurable, so we dwell on it. Then we find that we have gone on to commit the sin. With temptation, resistance must be exerted at the first point of contact.

The kind of self-understanding that helps us resist temptation may be acquired in several ways. One way is through the *prayerful study of the Word of God.* James 1:22–25 describes the Bible as a mirror in which we see ourselves. There we see the standards of the Christian life as set forth by God and exemplified and illustrated by Jesus. We may measure ourselves against these standards. We also see descriptions and illustrations of the same kinds of sins to which we fall prey. Our study of the Word should, as in all other things, be accompanied by prayer for divine illumination and understanding. The psalmist prayed, "Search me, O God, and know my heart; test me and know my anxious thoughts. See if there is any offensive way in me, and lead me in the way everlasting" (Ps. 139:23–24). This is a prayer we ought to pray often. It will be answered.

Second, we may learn from our *experiences.* As we reflect back upon the times that we have succumbed to temptation and those times when we have successfully resisted, a pattern sometimes emerges. We ought to learn from the painful experiences that there are some areas of life in which we must stay clear of any possible danger.

Third, we can learn from the *insight of others.* Others often see us more clearly than we see ourselves. If Christian fellowship means anything, it should mean that other believers are able to help us understand ourselves so that we can better resist or even avoid temptation.

Know Your Enemy

A second essential for withstanding temptation is to know the enemy. Anyone engaged in any type of contest with an opponent seeks to know the opponent. Our country constantly keeps our enemies and potential enemies under surveillance. Similarly, other nations are observing us regularly. The same is true in sports. On any Saturday during the fall, men sit in the stands of major college football stadiums taking notes and drawing diagrams. They are not there primarily to enjoy the game. They are scouts from future opponents of one or both teams.

Preparation for a successful contest includes knowing the nature and workings of the opponent. Jesus was able to resist the devil because he recognized him for what he was: an enemy, not merely a potential friend offering helpful advice (which is how the devil's suggestion about turning the stones into loaves of bread could have been interpreted).

We need to know the enemy's *appearance.* Peter says he sometimes comes as a roaring lion, seeking someone to devour (1 Pet. 5:8). This is his "hard sell," the fierce opposition. At other times he is more subtle, pictured as masquerading as an angel of light (2 Cor. 11:14). This is his "soft sell." He comes subtly, gently planting seemingly harmless and sensible-sounding suggestions in our minds: "Go ahead. You owe it to yourself." Or perhaps, "Don't be old-fashioned. Everyone does it these days." Here he is less easily recognized, and therefore perhaps more dangerous. Satan probably does not care for publicity, nor does he desire to be recognized. In some cases, it best serves him not to be.

Second, we must *know the enemy's method* of working, *his point of attack.* Usually this will be at the point of our weakness. As we observed earlier, it is especially important that we know and understand ourselves. At other times he attacks at our point of apparent strength. We usually think of Abraham as the paragon of faith. On at least two occasions, though, he presented Sarah as his sister rather than his wife, apparently because he was unable to believe that Jehovah could preserve and protect him. We do not picture Peter lacking courage and boldness. He even took up weapons against the group that came to take Jesus. Yet when a young woman asked him if he was one of Jesus' disciples, he denied that he even knew the Lord. These men of God were perhaps overconfident about their strengths. As a result, their strength actually became a weakness.

We must also *be aware of Satan's limitation.* He wants us to believe that he is virtually all-powerful, that we cannot resist him. He is powerful, more powerful than we are in our unaided strength, but he is not all-powerful. He could tempt Job only to the extent that God permitted him. He could not exceed those limits. The scriptural promise is: "And God is faithful; he will not let you be tempted beyond what you can bear. But when you are tempted, he will also provide a way out so that you can stand up under it" (1 Cor. 10:13). Although our enemy is stronger than we are, he is not stronger than we and God together: "The one who is in you is greater than the one who is in the world" (1 John 4:4). Sin is avoidable. We should not be intimidated by the seemingly overwhelming force of evil. Sometimes we depersonalize the idea, but it is still basically the same: "I couldn't help myself. It's just the way I was brought up," or "It's in my genes. It's just how I am." It need not be so.

Live In and Live Out the Bible

Third, in order to withstand temptation we must know the Bible. In response to each temptation Jesus replied with Scripture from the Book of Deuteronomy. In each case, that settled the argument. Not only did Jesus believe in the authority of the Scriptures, but Satan accepted it as well. Because Jesus knew the Scriptures, he knew the appropriate answer to each temptation.

God has promised to provide us with a way of escape from temptation. One of these means is the Bible. If we really know the Word of God, we will know the answer to temptations that arise. When we are tempted to become discouraged, for example, we will find a real basis for encouragement in the psalmists' praise of God and reflection upon his greatness and glory. When we are tempted to the wrong kind of pleasure we will find help in Proverbs. When we experience doubt, the Gospel according to John can strengthen us. Sadness can be countered with Paul's specific instructions in Philippians 4. The reply to apathy or indifference is found in John's letters to the seven churches in Revelation 1–3.

We need to know the Bible. When temptation comes, we often do not have opportunity to consult our Bibles, or to look up verses in a concordance or topical Bible. Through thorough and regular reading of Scripture we will be so familiar with it that we will know what God has said on a given subject. We will know the "mind of the Lord."

We need to know both what the Bible *says* and what it *means*. We need to study it, with the aid of a study Bible, commentary, or Bible teacher. The reason is this. A portion of the Bible can be taken out of context and represented as saying something that it does not mean. Even Satan used the Scripture when he tempted Jesus. But Jesus knew the meaning of the Bible so thoroughly that he knew it did not mean what Satan represented it as saying. One of Satan's favorite methods of temptation today is the half-truth.

When I was a boy, we fished at a small lake near our home, using bamboo poles and worms. We were careful to cover the barb of the hook so that no part showed. What we were saying as we lowered that J-shaped worm into the water was, "See, fishy, here is a nice, juicy, delicious, nutritious worm." And that was certainly true. There was nothing wrong with the worms we used (fishing with artificial lures has always seemed somewhat immoral to me). But it wasn't the entire truth. The rest of it was: "There's a hook inside the worm, and if I get the opportunity, I will drive it through your upper jaw." We were careful not to advertise that portion of the truth. So is Satan. He presents partial truth, telling of the pleasure of sin and its rewards, which in the short term are sometimes quite impressive. He can sometimes find Scripture that seems to support this. But the rest of the truth, which he does not tell us, is that sin also leads to sorrow, suffering, and tragedy. If we know our Bibles well, we will know the full truth.

Depend on the Father

We must know our heavenly Father. Before his series of temptations, Jesus had established his submission to the will of the Father by his baptism. On the eve of his greatest trial, Jesus prayed intensely and at length in the garden of Gethsemane. He knew where to turn in time of need: to his Father. Jesus was fully God and without sin, but he restricted the exercise of his deity by adding full humanity to it. He functioned in dependence upon the Father. If he found it necessary to depend upon the Father, how much more must we.

Human children learn to turn to their parents when they are in need. In our family there was a neat division of labor. Scraped-up knees and elbows were taken to Mom; broken toys and other similar problems were directed to Dad, in the belief that anything could be repaired with Scotch tape and Elmer's glue. As children we turn for help to someone larger, wiser, stronger than ourselves; this should also be true in spiritual matters. When temptation comes, if we remember to pause for a moment and pray, "God, help me!" we would often find the way of escape that he has provided. The availability of the way of escape will depend upon the nature of the relationship we have maintained with God. When we need his deliverance, there often will not be time and opportunity to restore a relationship we have neglected. It is best to have an ongoing relationship with him, so that we are friends, not strangers. God does not want us to have merely a "customers' relationship," in which we come to him only in times of need. He wants us to have a "social relationship," to be his friends.

These are the four ways Jesus resisted temptation. Temptation is a contest in which there are no ties, draws, or no "contests." One party is the winner and the other the loser. Temptation is a stairway on which we either ascend in victory to greater strength, or descend in defeat. The picture at the end of Matthew 4:1–11 shows the devil departing, utterly defeated, and Jesus being ministered to by the angels. And so it will also be for us if we use the resources God has provided.

Put It into Practice

There are several steps you can follow to assure that the temptations that inevitably come into your life do not necessarily lead to sin:

1. Familiarize yourself with the way in which Satan tempts believers by studying instances of temptation in the Bible. Read a book such as C. S. Lewis's *Screwtape Letters.*

2. Resist temptation at the first point of suggestion by thrusting the idea away. Be careful about your fantasy life, about dwelling on the idea of the sinful action in your imagination.

3. Avoid situations in which you will be exposed to temptations to which you are especially vulnerable.

4. When you do succumb to temptation and sin, ask yourself why that happened and how you can avoid yield-

ing to similar temptations in the future. Learn from your past mistakes.

5. Study God's promises and instructions about various types of temptations. Use a concordance or a topical Bible to identify these.

6. Study the ways in which men and women in the Bible successfully resisted temptation, as contrasted with those who yielded to sin. Why was Joseph, for example, able to resist a more active and persistent temptation to sexual immorality than that of David, who sinned?

7. Seek to determine your points of special vulnerability to temptation by examining your own heart and experience, and by praying that the Holy Spirit will give you self-understanding and discernment.

Study Guide

Key Concept Questions

1. According to the author, the believer can success-fully resist temptation if he or she correctly under-stands the factors at work in temptation and acts upon this knowledge. Specifically, in what four areas do we need to concentrate in order to more fully understand these factors?
2. What are three ways that believers can acquire the kind of self-understanding that will enable them to resist temptation?
3. In what three ways are believers to "know the enemy"?
4. In order to successfully "live in and live out the Bible," we need to know not only what the Bible says but what it means. How should we go about finding the correct meaning?

Bible Investigation

Consider the very first surrender to temptation as recorded in Genesis 3. Analyze Adam and Eve's response to this temptation in light of the four areas of awareness that the author suggests are needed to successfully resist temptation. Did Adam and Eve acknowledge their vul-nerability? Did they recognize the enemy? Did they under-stand the instructions God gave them? Did they seek out God when they were tempted? Turn now to the story of Joseph's temptation in Genesis 39. Analyze Joseph's response in light of these same four areas of awareness.

Personal Life Application

Reflect on Matthew 4:1–11, describing Jesus' tempta-tion by Satan. In what ways was Jesus particularly vul-nerable to temptation at this time? When in your own life are you apt to be particularly vulnerable to tempta-tion? It is important to realize that Satan is constantly trying to get at our weak spots, not only at times when we are the weakest, but also when we seem to be successfully operating from a position of strength. Read through the account of Samson's life in Judges 13–16. When was he especially vulnerable to temptation? (note Judges 14:1–3; 16:1, 4).

For Further Thought

Idea A

The author states that success in resisting temptation is dependent in part on knowing the nature and workings of the opponent, Satan. We cannot really appreciate the subtlety of Satan's methodology without first acquiring a clear concept of the essential nature of sin. Re-read the account of Adam and Eve's sin in Genesis 3. Then turn to the account of Moses' sin in Number 20:1–13. Try to determine from these two accounts the essence of sin. In other words, what was the real sin committed in each of these cases? What is Satan's motivation in continuing to tempt believers?

Idea B

Consider the phrase in the Lord's Prayer, "and lead us not into temptation." Does this suggest that it is God who leads us into temptation? Why or why not? (see James 1:13–15 and Job 1). Now read the parallel accounts of David taking the census from 2 Samuel 24 and 1 Chronicles 21. How can you explain the difference in the way each of these two accounts reports the one responsible for inciting David's action to take the census?

6

The Hidden Value of Doubt

Luke 7:18–30

When my wife knows that I'm bringing home guests for dinner, sometimes she gives me special instructions: "When you come, park the car in front and bring them in the front door. Don't bring them in through the garage!"

Now of course there is nothing illegal or immoral in our garage. But there are times when our garage is not very presentable. It is occasionally a mess! Only our best friends—who have seen our garage and whose garages we have seen—are brought through that area. Perhaps there is a bedroom or a closet in your house that you wouldn't want someone to see.

Our lives have untidy places, too. Tucked away in the crevices where no one can see them are experiences and aspects of our character that we don't want others to observe. There are sins, weaknesses, failures. One thing that we frequently hide from public sight is doubt.

For many of us, at one time or another the question arises, "Is it really true? Is the Christian faith simply a myth, a tradition that has been passed on, which I have uncritically accepted? Is it simply something that I was taught as a child, but which may be untrue?" Sometimes our doubt applies to a specific teaching of Christian belief; at other times, to the whole system.

We tend to hide doubt because we think it an awful and shameful thing—something that a "good Christian" does not experience. We need to see doubt from the correct perspective. It is not the same as disbelief or unbelief. It is *an occasion* that gives us the possibility of either disbelief or stronger faith. Its relationship to disbelief is similar to the relationship of temptation to sin. Doubt will come. (I do not say, as some do, that we ought to seek it.) We may not be able to prevent its arrival, and we are not responsible for its coming. What happens after it arrives, however, is up to us.

Doubt came to even such a great man as John the Baptist, whom Jesus spoke of in incomparable terms (Luke 7:28). Some teachers suggest that it was not John who was troubled by doubt, probably because they want to protect his reputation against the charge of having experienced uncertainty. They say it was John's disciples who doubted, and that he sent them to Jesus to receive evidence and confirmation for their faith. From my reading of Luke 7:18–30, however, I note that Jesus instructed those two messengers to go and *tell John what they saw and heard* (v. 22). The lesson we are to learn from Luke 7:18–30 is the way John dealt with doubt. If we handle it as John did, it can become constructive and strengthening in our lives.

Doubt Occurs Where There Is Legitimate Risk

The first step in dealing with doubt is to understand that it stems from risk. While there are generally other factors, such as the presence of some external threat to belief, doubt occurs when something is being genuinely risked upon the truth of what is believed. It seems strange to hear John the Baptist ask, "Are you the one?" Can this be the same man who announced the coming of the Messiah in clear terms: "He is the one who comes after me, the thongs of whose sandals I am not worthy to untie" (John 1:27)? On the basis of this belief, he preached a firm and pointed message of repentance, warning his hearers to flee from the coming wrath. When Jesus appeared, John identified him clearly and definitely: "Look, the Lamb of God, who takes away the sin of the world" (1:29). In all of this he showed no uncertainty, no equivocation. His message was sure and definite. How could things have changed so radically that John's "He is!" became, "Are you?" How could the exclamation point have been bent into a question mark? To understand this we have to see John's circumstances at the time.

At this point John was in prison for his fearless preaching, which even included a condemnation of Herod for his evil actions. John was no longer able to carry on an active ministry, and he probably sensed that he would never leave prison alive, an apprehension that proved to be true. He realized that his espousal and declaration of the message that Jesus was the Messiah was no trivial matter. He was to give his very life for this belief. In this situation it is not surprising that he experienced doubt. Our need for certainty is in direct proportion to the seriousness of our commitment to something—to what we have risked upon its truth. Where little is risked, there is little need for certainty and consequently little likelihood of doubt.

Some people are seldom if ever troubled by doubt, for various reasons. For some, it is because there is really very little at stake. People who spend one hour per week in church when it's convenient, throw an occasional dollar in the offering plate, and live during the rest of the week just as if they did not believe the Christian message are not likely to experience much doubt. What if their belief is false? They lose practically nothing. On the other hand, consider those who take Christ more seriously, who give themselves to the call and tasks of the

Lord, who forego pleasures that they otherwise might enjoy. If they are wrong they have thrown away their lives, or at least wasted part of them. You would expect them to ask themselves, "Is it all true, or have I made a great mistake?"

This need for security can be seen in more mundane areas of human experience as well. If you show me a rope and tell me that you are going to use it to suspend me two feet above the ground, I will probably say without hesitation, "Give me the rope." If you tell me that you will use the rope to support me two thousand feet above the ground, I will have some doubts. I will probably examine every inch of it, perhaps even x-ray it to make sure that there are no hidden breaks in the inner strands. In the former case, if the rope breaks the worst that can happen is a moderate bump. In the latter, my very life is at stake.

I find this tendency to need extra security for what I normally take for granted appearing in rather bizarre fashion at times. When I mail a letter I ordinarily give little thought to what happens after I drop it in the mail slot. When I mail a particularly important letter, though, sometimes I drop it in the opening, start toward my car, then go back and open the lid to make sure the letter has dropped down. Similarly, I ordinarily set the clock radio, turn the knob, and climb into bed without hesitation. But when I have an especially important engagement, I sometimes get into bed knowing I have turned the knob, and yet get up to check the clock. I may even do it more than once.

When we are taking our Christian faith seriously and trying to live as committed disciples, if we sometimes find ourselves lacking assurance that our faith is valid, we should not be ashamed. It is natural for doubt to occur when we risk something for our faith.

Confront Your Doubts with Evidence

Doubt is satisfied by evidence. John did the right thing. He sent his disciples to Jesus to inquire whether he really was the one. John could have tried to resolve the issue himself. Instead, he went to the source, to the one who had made these fantastic claims. And he was not disappointed, for the Lord welcomes each honest inquiry.

Jesus might have condemned John. He might have said, "You'd better stop asking questions like this. If you don't cease this damnable doubting, you're going to lose your salvation and your soul." That would have stopped John from asking questions, or at least from directing them to Jesus. Or Jesus might have asserted his authority. He might have said, "Yes, tell John that I am he." This would have put pressure on John. It would have accentuated John's problem. He would have had to make his decision based on the bare authority of Jesus' word, without supporting evidence of any kind. Jesus had a perfect right to do this. He is Lord. His word is perfect truth and therefore fully authoritative. He could have insisted that his word be accepted or rejected on its own basis.

Jesus could have responded to John's request in a condescending way that made John wish he hadn't asked. In so doing Jesus would have suggested that John really should not need this support, that his faith was second-rate. Or he might have taken the nondirective approach, simply echoing John's feelings: "I understand, John. You are uncertain about these matters of belief. I hear you saying that you are having second thoughts about who I am." That might have helped John's feelings temporarily, but it would not have solved his longer-term problem.

But Jesus didn't give any of these responses. He gave John the basis he needed to make a decision. He presented the evidence by pointing to what he was doing, and let John decide for himself. In so doing he showed respect for John as a person. He did not overwhelm him with indisputable proof. In effect, he said to John, "Here is the evidence: what I am doing. Now you decide for yourself whether I am the one."

To the person who honestly desires to know and is willing to act upon the evidence, the Lord offers a sufficient basis for belief. It is not so complete that we cannot still disbelieve. It is always subject to the possibility of other interpretations, so that we may disbelieve. But our Lord is compassionate. He understands our human frailty because he was fully human. Occasions of doubt certainly came to him during his earthly ministry. And he makes it possible for us to believe.

Wise Christians, when experiencing doubt, will do what John did. They will seek an answer to their questions by examining the Bible and praying that God will make clear the ground of faith. Sometimes our prayer may even have to be, "God—if there is a god—make yourself known to me." We will share our concern with our pastor or some other specially trained Christian. We will ask for reading suggestions, because there are a wealth of books that deal with the evidences for Christianity. And we will act upon the evidences provided.

The late Bertrand Russell, atheistic philosopher and author of *Why I Am Not a Christian*, was once asked what would be necessary for him to believe in God. Russell replied, "If a voice were to come from the sky, predicting very unlikely events, and some time later they occurred, then I would believe." But I wonder about the sincerity of his statement. Christianity's claim of biblical prophecy is that this has actually taken place. God does not write across the sky each morning in fifteen-foot-high block letters. "THERE IS A GOD," but he has provided evidence for us to believe, if we are willing.

From Jesus' response to John we can also learn how to treat questioners. Sometimes children and teens in the church are turned off by usual adult responses to questions about how they handle their doubts: authoritarian response, evasion of a pious "just believe."

In the early 1900s a young man named Nels Ferré came to America from Sweden. His father was a Baptist pastor

DOES IT MATTER HOW I LIVE?

of the old school, and Nels was a bright, sensitive boy who had questions about the faith. When he went to his father with these questions, he regularly received one piece of advice: "Don't ask such questions!" His autobiography tells how he cried himself to sleep at night, out of concern for the damned who were suffering in hell. It also describes his three conversions: first to orthodox Christianity, second to honesty, and third to love.

Nels decided that orthodox Christianity and honesty were incompatible. His pastor, who later became theology professor at Bethel Seminary, said, "It was a tragedy that we lost him." Nels went on to become one of America's foremost theologians, but with a theology that was far from the evangelical faith in which he was reared, especially in his view of the person of Christ.

You Can Get in Control of Your Doubts

Doubt is subject to voluntary control. Jesus seemed to hold people responsible for whether or not they believed. That is why his final comment to John the Baptist was, "Blessed is the man who does not fall away on account of me" (Luke 7:23). Jesus commended John's belief and condemned the Pharisees who rejected his word. In Luke 7:29–30 the two reactions are vividly contrasted. In Jesus' view, a person either believed or disbelieved because of personal choice.

But how can this be? We do not turn our belief on and off any more than we can turn our emotions on and off by deciding to do so. If the latter were the case, few people would ever be sad. We do not directly control our feelings by an act of the will; similarly, we do not simply choose to believe or disbelieve. What we are able to do is to choose what we are going to focus our attention on. John could have decided to concentrate on the facts of his imprisonment: cells, walls, chains, locks, and guards. If he had done this, he certainly would have settled down into unbelief. On the other hand, if he chose to dwell on the report his disciples brought back, his faith would be satisfied and strengthened. Judging from the words of commendation that Jesus spoke about John, he apparently focused on the faith-building facts.

We can select what we are going to give our primary attention to. We need to look for the evidence where it has been promised. Sometimes a scientifically minded person says, "There is no God. I don't find him with my scientific method." This is like a man drawing a net through the water. Because the holes are large he catches no fish. He declares, "There are no fish here," but all he has proved is that there are no fish large enough to get caught in his net. God is not the kind of being who can be found through the scientific method.

Gherman Titov, one of the earliest Russian cosmonauts, returned from his spaceflight and announced, "I didn't see God up there." Christians have never claimed that God could be reached and seen through space travel. But there is experiential, historical, philosophical, and scientific evidence supporting the truth claims of Christianity, and the honest inquirer will look there. Aristotle wrote, "It is the mark of an educated man to look for precision in each class of things just so far as the nature of the subject admits." There is evidence, if we are willing to look where God has put it.

There is one further dimension to the volitional character of doubt. Doubt may be moral as well as intellectual. I recall the dismay I felt when talking to a specific man about the Christian faith. He seemed to accept all of the elements of faith, until I asked him if he would like to become a Christian. His answer was firm and clear: "No. Because if Christianity is true and I accept these things, I will have to make some radical changes in the way I live, and I don't want to do that." The Lord is looking for people who are both open-minded and open-hearted.

Doubt will come to us, but it is up to us to determine what it does to us. If, like John, we are wise enough to

DOES IT MATTER HOW I LIVE?

understand the nature and cause of doubt, to bring it to the Lord for his evidence, and to focus upon the positive evidence he gives, then we too will find our faith made even stronger through the tests we face.

Put It into Practice

Here are some steps you can take to deal successfully with doubt, so that it strengthens rather than weakens your faith:

1. Recognize that doubt is a normal occurrence in the life of even the strongest believer, and that it is not the same as unbelief.

2. Bring your doubt honestly to Jesus, asking him to strengthen your faith.

3. Study portions of Scripture, such as the Gospel of John, which were written especially to build faith.

4. Seek out someone, such as a pastor or Bible teacher, who can point you to some of the evidences supporting faith.

5. If your doubt is centered in a specific area, such as science or politics, find a dedicated Christian who is an expert in that area and ask him or her to help you deal with your questions.

6. Recognize that the teachings of Christianity, like many other important beliefs and values such as love and truth, are not of a scientific nature, but have their own confirmation appropriate to them.

7. Emphasize the positive rather than the negative aspects of life.

8. Face honestly the question of your willingness to do what would be required of you if the Bible teaching is true.

Study Guide

1. In what way is doubt different from disbelief or un-belief?
2. How is the element of risk related to the experiencing of doubt?
3. Describe the way that Jesus responded to the uncertainty expressed by John the Baptist in Luke 7.
4. What technique does the author suggest that we use in order to get doubt under control?

Bible Investigation

Listed below are some individuals for whom doubt played a part in their willingness to trust God. Investigate each case and describe not only the occasion in which doubt arose, but also how God responded to each doubter. Why does it appear that God was less patient in Zechariah's case? Collectively, what can we learn from these examples about God's response to our doubts?

Abraham	Genesis 17:17
Sarah	Genesis 18:9–15
Moses	Exodus 3–4
Israelites	Exodus 16
Gideon	Judges 6
Zechariah	Luke 1
Thomas	John 20:24–30

Personal Life Application

Sometimes Christians find it difficult to continue to simply "believe" when everything in their world is falling apart—when a job has been lost, when relationships have gone sour, or when health has deteriorated. Imagine that you have a friend who has undergone an extended period of suffering, and who begins to express to you some doubts concerning God's caring for him or her. How would you go about comforting your friend in such a way as to help satisfy some of these doubts? You may wish to refer to James 1:1–18 and Mark 9:14–29.

For Further Thought

Idea 1

The author makes the dual assertion that "doubt is subject to voluntary control," and yet "we do not turn our belief on and off any more than we can turn our emotions on and off by deciding to do so." How can these two seemingly contradictory statements be reconciled? Again, refer to James 1:1–8 and Mark 9:14–24.

Idea 2

The author suggests, by this chapter title, that there is a positive aspect of doubt, a "hidden value." How can this be, in view of the fact that doubting is sometimes rebuked in Scripture?

7

How to Know You Know God's Will

Acts 16:1–10

Imagine you are in an airplane. Your seatbelt is fastened and your serving tray is in the normal position. Soothing music is playing over the headphones.

You've already read the travel magazine, and all you can see from the window is water, from horizon to horizon. You gaze at the blue expanse below, amazed at its breadth. Then after a few more minutes you see something on the horizon. It's a mountain, thrusting up from an island. As you gradually get closer the mountain looms larger and larger, dominating the northern end of the island, which itself is beginning to spread. *That's it*, you think. *Mount Fuji*.

Later, your plane touches down at Nerima International Airport. You soon find yourself in the streets of downtown Tokyo. It is a beautiful day, and the streets are crowded with people. But you are not at your final destination. You have to find a particular house on a specific street in a certain suburb. How will you find it?

There is an abundance of information around you. You could ask someone on the street for directions, but the problem is you wouldn't understand a word you heard. Here you are, with an abundance of information *available* to guide you, but it is not *accessible*. You don't know how to find its meaning.

Sometimes we Christians find ourselves in a similar situation. We want to know the Lord's will, so we can do it. God has promised to guide us in all that we do, and so all around us we find indications of his guidance. But unless we know how to understand and interpret these communications, they are of no effective value to us. Our problem is finding an answer to the question: How do I determine God's will for me?

The Bible gives us God's promise that he will guide us into his will. In Proverbs 3:5–6 we read: "Trust in the LORD with all your heart and lean not on your own understanding; in all your ways acknowledge him, and he will make your paths straight." Jesus told those who questioned the authority of his teaching, "If anyone chooses to do God's will, he will find out whether my teaching comes from God or whether I speak on my own." How can I identify and interpret that guidance for my living today?

While God's promise that he will guide believers is genuine, knowing his will is not simple. Rev. Alan Redpath, who at the time was pastor of Moody Memorial Church in Chicago, was seeking God's will about a call he had received from another congregation. In the midst of his struggles he remembered that he had written a book on the subject of knowing God's will. Thinking that it might help him, he re-read the book but found it gave him little assistance.

In practice, how does guidance come to the believer? By what means did God actually direct believers during biblical times? Let's consider four channels of God's guidance.

Look for Guidance in the Bible

One channel of guidance is the Word of God. This should be the first place the Christian turns because today God reveals himself primarily in the Bible.

Some of the issues that we face are so directly, clearly, and definitely spoken about in the Bible that we will not have to look any further. For example, the Bible excludes certain types of occupations as viable options for Christians. Certain ways of relating to people are commended, even commanded, by God in the Bible. Sometimes it may be difficult to determine whether the course of action we are considering is a suggestion or a command. But once we determine this, we have the answer to the question, "What should I do?"

The question here is simply whether we are willing to do what God commands. We occasionally bemoan the fact that there are parts of the Bible that we do not understand, and consequently cannot act upon. But probably for most of us there are considerable portions of the Bible that we do understand and are not obeying. For me, as I suppose for most Christians, it often is the parts of the Bible I do understand, rather than those I do not understand, which really cause me problems.

In practice, the Bible does not give explicit commands for resolving a large percentage of the problems we face. One reason for this is that many of the issues we consider are far too specific to be dealt with in the Bible. If this were not the case, we would not be able to carry a Bible around under our arms or in our pockets. It would be so large that we would need a truck or even a moving van to carry it around with us.

The other difficulty is that some of the issues we face today were not present in the biblical era. We live in a more highly developed, complex society than did the ancient Hebrews. They did not have to wrestle with moral dilemmas such as mechanically prolonged life, AIDS, surrogate parenting, and nuclear summits. Conversely, some of the issues that perplexed people in biblical times are not present for us today. Because the Bible was written first to a specific people in specific times and places, it may not give us a one-step solution to our problems. We may not be able to take what was commanded in biblical times and simply follow it today in unmodified form. Nonetheless, many biblical teachings declare principles that we can follow. And there are many narratives that embody principles upon which we can build. These principles are permanent and we can apply them to our present situations. Here you'll find most of your biblical direction.

Some of these principles are quite general in nature, potentially applicable to every kind of situation. One of the questions Christians can ask when trying to determine God's will is, "What would Christ do?" First John 2:6 says, "Whoever claims to live in him must walk as Jesus did." As Christians we should familiarize ourselves with what Jesus actually said and did. From this we will often be able to conceive of what Jesus would have done, were he in our particular situation. A second question to ask is, "Will this glorify God?" In 1 Corinthians 10:31, Paul wrote, "So whether you eat or drink or whatever you do, do it all for the glory of God." Before making decisions we can ask, "If I do this, and am identified as belonging to God, will this bring glory to him, or will it discredit him and his kingdom?"

A third question is whether we can do something in the name of Jesus, as Paul wrote in Colossians 3:17: "And whatever you do, whether in word or deed, do it all in the name of the Lord Jesus, giving thanks to God the Father through him." As I contemplate a course of action, can I say that I do it in Jesus' name? Can I say I am doing this as Jesus' representative? Could I ask him to bless what I am doing? This focuses a penetrating scrutiny upon many of my contemplated actions.

Concern for the other person is also of great importance. Jesus said that the second great commandment is,

"You shall love your neighbor as yourself." In particular, Christians ask themselves about the influence that their actions will have on others. Paul was resolved that he would not even do what otherwise would be good, if it would harm his brother. He said, "Therefore, if what I eat causes my brother to fall into sin, I will never eat meat again, so that I will not cause him to fall" (1 Cor. 8:13). Christians act in ways that influence the spiritual development of other people positively, not negatively.

There also are principles growing out of specific types of cases. Some of these principles are the value of human life, the value of truth, the right of property. Christians will inquire which of these apply to the case they are considering and then apply them. For example, although the Bible does not address the question of speeding or driving after drinking alcoholic beverages, it does state the principle of the value of human life (Gen. 9:6) and the responsibility for caring respect versus negligence (Exod. 21:28–36). Studying a good book on biblical ethics will help us learn more about these specific principles.

Ask the Spirit for Help

The second channel of God's guidance is the indwelling Holy Spirit. Jesus promised his disciples that when the Holy Spirit came, he would guide them into all the truth. Since Pentecost, the Holy Spirit has come into the life of each person at conversion (1 Cor. 12:13) and lives within that individual from then on. As the Bible is God's means of guiding Christians from outside, the Holy Spirit is his means of guiding us from within. Negatively, this means that as Christians we must be willing to let the Spirit direct us, that we must be certain that we are not placing an obstruction in the Spirit's way. This relationship is like a dual-control automobile, in which we have one set of controls and the Holy Spirit has the other. Our controls can always override his. Hence, unless we are careful to seek his will and his guidance, his purposes for us will be stifled. We will take control and go out of control. The Bible is like a mirror. Sometimes I see myself mirrored in rather unflattering (but accurate) fashion, as in Psalm 32:9, "Do not be like the horse or the mule, which have no understanding but must be controlled by bit and bridle or they will not come to you." When I am like that, the Holy Spirit cannot work.

Positively, however, to be guided by the Spirit of God we must practice or develop his guidance in our thinking and willing. This is done by permitting him to have access to the very center of our consciousness. I believe that we can do it something like this. We pray to the Holy Spirit, telling him that we want to be guided by him, and asking him to direct and even create our thoughts. Then we simply let our minds go limp. We do not consciously try to produce thoughts. We let him bring ideas, feelings, and impressions to our minds. This is a practice that few Americans know much about. We are so activistic that we must be constantly doing something. We must have external stimulation. Consequently, some of the Eastern religions have moved into the vacuum created by Western Christianity's neglect, and have introduced nonbiblical forms of meditation that allow forces other than God to fill the mind. If we have properly prepared ourselves to listen to God, and have asked the Holy Spirit to direct our thinking, we can be confident that he will do so.

When a TV screen has the horizontal hold out of adjustment, we see a confusing maze of colored flashes, shaking crazily and tearing diagonally. We cannot make out the picture clearly. Then we turn a knob and make a slight adjustment. Suddenly the mad tearing, jerking, flashing, and convulsing cease, the picture locks into place, and what was a confused and incomprehensible image before is now clearly seen. Sometimes life's experiences appear that way—a confused mass of ideas, feelings, hopes, and fears. We cannot see clearly the picture of what we are to do. Then the Holy Spirit takes control, the picture locks into place, and we see and understand his will. It is a wonderful promise that God has given us the Holy Spirit's guidance, and a promise that we are privileged to use.

Read Your Circumstances Carefully

A third channel of divine guidance is God's control and direction of circumstances. He is the Lord of history and can govern the circumstances of life in a way that makes clear what he intends for us. The Bible is full of cases of God's circumstantial leading. The most famous case is Gideon, for whom God made the fleece wet and the ground around it dry, and then the fleece dry when the surrounding earth was wet. Perhaps a more relevant case is in Acts 16:7, where we read that although Paul and his companions attempted to go into Bithynia, the Spirit of Jesus did not allow them to do so. Then Paul received a vision in the night of a man calling them to come to Macedonia and help the people there. In Galatians 4:13, Paul indicated that it was because of a bodily ailment that he first preached in Galatia, a Macedonian city. This may have been the restraint that kept him in Galatia preaching the Word. Our circumstances often indicate what our Lord has in mind for us.

We need to be careful here. At this point our danger of superstition is greatest. It comes, when we try to prescribe to God what circumstances he must use, and what these circumstances will mean. Suppose I am trying to decide whether God wants me to do A or B. I pray, "Lord, if you want me to do A, let it be raining when I arrive at church on Sunday morning, but if you want me to do B, cause the sun to shine brightly." At the same time a fellow worshiper prays, "Lord, if you want me to do C, then have the sun shine brightly at worship time this Sunday morning, and if your will for me is D, send rain then." Now what if God wants me to do A and wants my friend to do C? What can he do about the weather? I have no doubt that, being almighty, God can enable me to experience rain while my friend sees sunshine, but this seems to place a ridiculous burden upon God. Frankly, it is a trap that stems from a self-centered outlook, ignoring the fact that God has millions of believers whom he is trying to guide.

I once heard a Christian professor say that when he was a student he prayed at one point that if God wanted him to follow a certain course of action he should show him this by causing him to get an A grade in one of the courses that he was taking. That seems to me to be a type of spiritual blackmail. It is much better to let God decide upon the circumstances and illuminate us to understand which ones are significant, and what they mean. Gideon seemed to do the prescribing, but Gideon lived in a period in which there was not a continuous personal presence of the Holy Spirit in the lives of believers. When the Spirit came upon a person for a definite purpose, he came powerfully and controllingly, and he undoubtedly inspired in Gideon the idea of choosing that particular sign.

What we need to do instead is to pray that God will control the circumstances as he wills, and help us to see how he is working in these circumstances. Then he is able to use these as factors in his total working. Note that I have placed this element of knowing God's will third, after the Bible and the Holy Spirit, in the proper order of precedence.

God generally works through circumstances in ways that make sense to us. We can see life's circumstances nudge us, sometimes gently, sometimes forcefully, in the direction in which he wants us to go. A person who becomes seriously ill in certain climates is probably not being led to live where these climates prevail. A student who does very poorly in science is likely not being directed by God into the medical profession as his or her life work. God is an almighty God, and he can work in ways that would be rather unlikely for mere human effort. But usu-

DOES IT MATTER HOW I LIVE?

ally when he does that, he will also make clear to us that he is dealing with us in an exceptional fashion.

Listen to What Others Counsel

The fourth and final channel of God's guidance is through the counsel of other godly believers. The Bible contains many instances of one believer helping another discern God's will. Jethro's counsel to Moses (Exod. 18:17–23) is one example. A more forceful one is Paul's encounter with Peter (Gal. 2:14). Today, God still uses other people to help us recognize his leading. Notice that I use the expressions "help another discern, or recognize." That is the role of other Christians: not to discover God's will for us and tell it to us, but to help us see it for ourselves. God reveals his will for me to *me*, and for you to *you*. I am always uneasy with people who seem to feel they know God's will for me or anyone else.

There are several reasons why another Christian can be of help. The other person, especially a more mature and experienced Christian, may well know Scriptures that you don't and can call these to your attention. The other person may have experienced situations similar to what you are facing. You may recognize in the way God dealt with him or her parallels to what you are experiencing. Or, simply because the other person is not you, he or she is not quite so close to the factors in the problem, not so emotionally involved with the issues as you are. He or she can consequently see some things more clearly than you can.

I recall a pastor who was trying to determine what to do about a number of situations in his church. He went to another pastor who knew both him and the church fairly well and shared his situation with the other pastor. The first man reported, "He was able to see clearly some things that I was too close to see." This is the role of other Christians in helping us find God's will. They are not people who look through a microscope or telescope and tell us what we could see there. Rather, they adjust and focus the scope for us, so we may more accurately see for ourselves.

If you who desire help in knowing God's will, seek out the wisest, most mature Christian you know whose judgment you trust and who will maintain confidentiality. It should be someone who is not personally involved in the issue. Sometimes this will be your pastor; at other times, another Christian. Through doing this you will find that there is real meaning to the idea of the body of Christ. God really does use other Christians as he guides you through life.

Are you willing to do God's will? If so, these words of Jesus echo down through time: "If anyone chooses to do God's will, he will find out whether my teaching comes from God."

Put It into Practice

Steps that will help you to recognize God's will are the following:

1. Study the Bible, especially focusing on the type of issue you are facing, using a topical Bible or a concordance. If the Bible does not seem to speak about your situation, ask yourself, "Are there problems spoken of in the Bible that resemble this situation or decision in significant ways?"

2. Ask whether the course of action you are considering seems to be more in agreement or disagreement with the principles that God has revealed in his Word, with the Scriptures that define his will and his purpose in the world. Does this glorify his name, help move others closer to him?

3. Pray for the guidance of the Holy Spirit. Tell him that you want him to have control of your thoughts and

feelings. Then, allow your mind to go blank, letting him have access to the inmost parts of your being.

4. Pray that God will not only guide you by directing the circumstances of your life, but will also illuminate your understanding about the significance of these circumstances.

Study Guide

Key Concept Questions

1. Name the four "channels" of God's guidance that the author identifies in this chapter. Should any one of these take precedence over the others? Why or why not?

2. What are some basic difficulties that arise when we try to use the Bible as a "handbook" for decision-making? In what "general" way does the author suggest that these difficulties can be surmounted?

3. List three questions that, when applied to our contemplated actions, can help us uncover some of the eternal biblical principles needed to guide us in a given decision-making situation.

Bible Investigation

Read two portions of Scripture, each providing us with information concerning guidance that Paul received when deciding upon places he should go to preach the gospel: Acts 16:1–10; and Romans 1:8–13. Identify the differences in the type of guidance provided in each situation. In which case was there clear evidence of "supernatural" guidance? To what extent do you think we should routinely depend on such supernatural manifestation in order to make decisions "according to God's will"? If we admit that supernatural communication is the exception rather than the rule, it would benefit us to more closely examine the Romans passage again. What does this passage have to teach us concerning the role of "planning" in the process of learning God's will? What does this passage have to say about the importance of establishing clear-cut goals? What role does prayer play? To what extent is it important to be able to adjust to the not-to-be-known-ahead-of-time aspects of God's will? After thinking through these questions, would you say that the application of wisdom is an appropriate method to use to discern God's will? Why or why not? (An important distinction to be made here is the nature of "heavenly" as opposed to "human" wisdom. See James 3:13–18.)

Personal Life Application

The author cautions that we should be very careful in using circumstances to give direction as to what God's will is in any given situation. In the Bible, the individuals who perhaps tried most to interpret circumstances were Job's friends. Yet no matter how hard they tried, they were unable to learn what was really going on or to advise Job appropriately. Circumstances can be very mysterious and therefore very easily misread. Read Ecclesiastes 11:1–6. From this passage draw some conclusions regarding the extent to which the interpreting of circumstances should influence our attempt to learn God's will. Then reflect upon a major decision that you are now making or have recently had to make. Analyze the extent to which you have allowed "circumstances" to dictate to you what you should do, in contrast to the amount of energy you have spent trying to identify and apply scriptural principles to the decision.

For Further Thought

The author states that

> to be guided by the Spirit of God we must practice or develop his guidance in our thinking and willing. This is done by permitting him to have access to the very center of our consciousness. I believe that we can do it something like this. We pray to the Holy Spirit, telling him that we want to be guided by him, and asking him to direct and even create our thoughts. Then we simply let our minds go limp.

Does this imply that all the mental work involved in identifying and applying scriptural principles to a decision should be discarded? Why or why not? If a friend claimed that he or she was confident that "the Lord was leading" him or her to make a certain decision, but the contemplated action violated a biblical principle, how would you evaluate that person's choice? Use John 14:26 to support your answer.

8

How to Be Confident You're Doing God's Will

Genesis 22:1–19

My telephone rang. A woman from my congregation was on the line. "Pastor," she said, "I wonder if sometime we could have a sermon on doing God's will. We talk a lot about it but it seems to me most of us do more talking than doing."

I did not ordinarily preach a sermon for the sake of one person. There are much more effective means of dealing with individual problems. But I preached that sermon because I sensed that her question and problem were not unique. Many of us, if we are honest with ourselves, have to admit that we know considerably more commands than we are obeying. There is a gap, a sort of "underlap," between our knowledge and performance. Yet the basic question of Christian living is how we can do the will of God.

Emil Brunner, a theologian of the early twentieth century said, "Faith is obedience, nothing more nor less." That is a bit oversimplified perhaps. Yet the Book of James suggests that Brunner's assessment is basically accurate: "You foolish man, do you want evidence that faith without deeds is useless? Was not our ancestor Abraham considered righteous for what he did when he offered his son Isaac on the altar? You see that his faith and his actions were working together, and his faith was made complete by what he did" (2:20–22).

We often think of Abraham as a model of faith. The proof of his faith was his obedience. Genesis 22:1–19 gives us an excellent example of the true nature of obedience, because Abraham was obedient in the face of a very difficult and painful command. Abraham's obedience demonstrates the essential factors for doing God's will.

To Do It, You Have to Know It

The first requisite to obedience is conviction of God's will. Unless we are really sure that something is what God wants us to do, we will never have the courage to do it. Genesis 22 begins very simply: "Some time later God tested Abraham." We then learn what God commanded. We are not told how God appeared or in what fashion he spoke. Possibly it was through an angelic visitor, as in the latter part of the passage. Whatever the means, Abraham knew without question that sacrificing Isaac was God's command. Without that conviction, he could never have done what he had to do. When he approached the moment of action, he would have engaged in the kind of self-searching that all sensitive people encounter in the face of moral dilemmas: "Is this really God's will, or is it simply my own idea?" With this sort of ambivalence, he could not have brought himself to attempt to take the life of his beloved son.

It may seem strange to us that Abraham could even conceive of an act of human sacrifice as possibly being God's will. The commandment, "You shall not murder" (Exod. 20:13), was not yet recorded, but the preservation of human life was commanded well before God gave the law (see Gen. 9:6, for example). We need to remember three factors, however. First, human sacrifice was quite common in that day. Around Abraham lived the worshipers of Moloch, who sacrificed their children to their god. Second, this was still early in God's self-revelation to the human race, and Abraham did not have the full understanding of God's moral law that we now have. Third, and most important, there is no indication that God ever intended Isaac to die. His intervention shows that. It was a test of Abraham's willingness to obey God. In principle it was no different than Jesus' teaching that his followers must "hate" their families for his sake.

To do God's will, like Abraham we need to be convinced that it is his will. Sometimes this requires taking extra time to reach conviction on a matter, but it is essential. We looked at "how" to know God's will in the previous chapter. The basic point is that knowing God's will must precede doing his will.

This is particularly important in view of the fact that God's will sometimes cuts across our own very important plans. It was certainly the case with Abraham. God had promised him a son. God made this promise when Abraham was seventy-five years of age and Sarah, his wife was sixty-five. Abraham had a long time to contemplate the birth of his heir. Isaac was born twenty-five years after God had first made the promise to his parents. During that time, Abraham had no doubt dreamed the dreams that he had previously abandoned, about what his son would be and do, how Isaac would work along with him and perhaps someday take his place. Isaac would be his security in old age.

Then Isaac was born. Abraham undoubtedly held the child in his arms many times and thought about how he would be the one through whom a great nation would come. And Abraham could think this way because he knew that God had promised this and had provided the child. But with the test from God, all his hopes, dreams, and expectations seemed about to be dashed.

We should not set our plans with such absoluteness and finality that we cannot allow the possibility that God's will may interfere with or alter our plans. If we have closed our minds in advance to certain possibilities, God will have a difficult time making his will clear to us. Abraham had definite plans and expectations, but they were not so firm that he could not consider and recognize God's leading. God's plan will not always fit our plans and desires. We need to be sensitive to his leading in unexpected directions.

I have disliked telegrams and long-distance telephone calls for a long time. On at least three occasions in my life, I thought I had things all worked out. I had projects planned, short- and long-range goals toward which I was aiming, and was proceeding steadily toward them. Then one of those telegrams or long-distance telephone calls cut right across my fine plans. In time I came to realize that this was God speaking to me, so I no longer resent those electrifying communications. I know rather that the problem lies with my too firmly fixed plans, and that I must learn to live with a sort of tentativeness that keeps me open to recognizing God's working in unexpected ways.

You Can Be Confident He Is Good

Second, in order to do God's will, you must be confident of God's goodness. This was a difficult challenge for Abraham. It would have been hard enough if the Lord had told him, "Take the knife and plunge it into Isaac immediately," but at least he could have carried out the act quickly. What made this test difficult was that he had to make preparations, and then take a three-day trip. He had three days to think about it—and it was probably almost impossible to think about anything else! As he rode the donkey, the force of each hoof striking the ground probably sent a tremor through Abraham, because he knew that it brought him another step nearer to the place where he must take Isaac's life.

The real moment of truth is described in verse 7. Abraham left his servants behind, with the comment, "I and the boy [will] go over there. We will worship and then we will come back to you." Abraham gave Isaac the wood to carry, while he took the flame and the knife. They had everything that they needed in order to offer the sacrifice, except the sacrificial animal.

Isaac was a perceptive young man. He turned to his father and asked, "The fire and the wood are here, but where is the lamb for the burnt offering?" Quite possibly he thought, *Am I to be the sacrifice?* How Isaac's question must have stabbed into Abraham's heart! And he had to answer, and answer truthfully. If he looked away, if he tried to say something he did not really believe, Isaac would know, because he knew his father. They had been close, and Isaac would be able to detect any insincerity. Abraham looked into his son's eyes and spoke what he truly believed: "God himself will provide the lamb for the burnt offering, my son" (v. 22:8). He was not merely encouraging his son or putting him at ease. He spoke his conviction here, just as he had when he told the servants, "I and the boy will go over there. We will worship, and then *we* will come back to you." But how could Abraham believe this in the absence of any supporting evidence?

The Bible doesn't tell us precisely what Abraham was thinking at this moment. Apparently he expected that God would provide the sacrificial animal. The writer of Hebrews suggests that Abraham possibly thought that Isaac would die, and then be restored to life again (Heb. 11:19). In any event, Abraham had no precise knowledge or proof of what would happen on the mountain, but he knew that God was a good God and that whatever happened there would be in keeping with the love, compassion, and mercy of God. God was not the type of being who enjoyed torturing those who were dedicated, submissive, and obedient to him. Abraham could trust Jehovah, not fear him.

This confidence was based upon his past experience with the Lord. He could think of his call to leave Ur of the Chaldees. Abraham had gone, not having seen the place where he was to go, but trusting God to provide. He had left behind all the security of his native land. And what had God done? Had he said, "Here's a man who will do whatever I ask of him. I'll really take advantage of him"? No, God had blessed him and made him a wealthy man. A time came when Abraham's herdsmen and those of his nephew contended for the grazing territories. Abraham stepped back and gave Lot the choice. Lot looked and saw the lush land of the Jordan Valley and chose that for himself. God honored Abraham for his unselfishness. He prospered him and gave him the promise of his posterity. Abraham knew from these experiences that God did not exploit his followers.

If we are to obey God, it will require that we know him well enough to realize that he is a loving, understanding, generous God whom we may trust, against whom we need not be on our guard. Then we will be willing to follow him no matter what, knowing that whatever his will may be, it will include our ultimate welfare.

In my home, we have a wall plaque. It is a wooden dinner plate with an inscription painted on it: "God always gives his best to those who leave the choice to him." This plaque is more than a decorative item. It is a basic part of the creed of the Erickson family, because we have found repeatedly in our experience that this is how God is and how he works. We've found him to be a good God.

A few years ago a young Christian family faced an important decision. They were engaged in a full-time ministry, but it seemed for some time that the Lord was ultimately leading them into another type of Christian service. The only question was when and where. Then one of those unexpected telephone calls came, and it appeared that this was indeed the time and place. They knew enough about the new ministry opportunity to know that it would involve some economic adjustment, some tightening of the budget. They were receiving a rather comfortable salary in their present position. They worked hard at paring down their budget, reasoning that they would not need to spend as much money on transportation, entertainment, and some other things. They arrived at a minimum figure, which they felt they needed, a figure more than 40 percent below what they were then receiving. Then they prayed, "Lord, if you want us to accept the position at a lesser figure, we know you'll provide, but this is what we feel we need to get along without too severe an adjustment." They entered into negotiations with the new institution, never mentioning the figure. When the position was officially offered to them it was at a salary more than 15 percent greater than the minimum they had arrived at. You could never convince this couple that God is not good to his followers.

True Obedience Is Always Complete

Third, in order to do the will of God, you must be completely obedient. Abraham did not falter partway through his act, nor did he try to alter the situation. He took the knife in his hand and would have plunged it into Isaac's body if the angel had not stopped him.

Many pressures could have deterred Abraham from full obedience. One was the possibility of being misunderstood. If Abraham had returned home without Isaac, he really could not tell anyone what had happened. Who would believe his wild story? People would gossip, "Abraham killed his son. He was jealous of Isaac, threatened by him, and so he killed him, and made up this wild story about his God commanding him to do this." If we are determined to do God's will, we must be prepared to be misunderstood. People will say things about us, and impute motives to us that we have never dreamed of. On one occasion when Jesus was preaching, his mother and brothers came to take him away quietly, apparently thinking he was out of his mind (Mark 3:21). Those who should have understood him best misunderstood him the most. Because we are likely to be misunderstood, we are tempted to substitute an incomplete act, a modification of God's will, for genuine obedience.

If Abraham had been inclined to do this he might have reasoned with God: "God, what good is a dead body to you? If you'll let me keep Isaac, I'll give you all my wealth, offer sacrifices to you, do anything that you may ask." The first king of Israel, Saul, attempted something like this, and the prophet Samuel came from the Lord, angrily bearing the message, "To obey is better than sacrifice" (1 Sam. 15:22). Unlike Saul, Abraham knew better than to attempt a substitution.

Abraham could have proposed an action that would produce the same end result, but by different means. He might have taken one of the servants up onto the mountain and commanded him to kill Isaac. The act would have been accomplished and by Abraham's decision, but he would have been spared carrying out the actual deed. This was not what Jehovah had commanded, and so Abraham did not suggest it.

We may think that some equivalent action may be substituted for complete obedience, but we do not know what seemingly insignificant detail is essential to what God is trying to do.

About twenty years ago a young man was studying in medical school because he believed God wanted him to be a medical missionary to a foreign land. As he thought about it, a new idea came to him. In all sincerity he prayed, "Lord, if I go to the mission field, I am only one worker. But if I remain in this country and set up a medical practice, I could give most of my income to your work, and maybe send three or four or more medical missionaries to the field." God in effect replied to him, "I didn't say anything to you about giving. I spoke to you about *going*." Today that man is a medical missionary. Completeness of obedience is essential to really doing God's will.

Upon Abraham's act of obedience, several things happened. Abraham's faith was strengthened. The next time God gave him a command, he could look back to God's provision and be more confident than ever. Isaac's faith was strengthened. He would never be the same again, having seen the goodness of the Lord. Jehovah knew that Abraham loved God more than even his own son (Gen. 22:12). Of course, God knew in advance what Abraham would do, but now both he *and* Abraham knew, and each knew that the other knew. And because of this the Lord was able to fulfill his promise, giving Abraham a great lineage, from whom one day the Savior came, bringing ultimate blessing to all who believe.

We will probably not be called to obedience quite as dramatically as Abraham. But the Lord has things for us to do, and our obedience is important. If with Abraham we are certain of God's will, have confidence in his goodness because of our experience of him, and are willing to be complete in our obedience, God will also enable us to do his will. And he will bless and use us as a result.

Put It into Practice

To be able to obey God, you need to:

1. Remember that God does not always work in the same way. His will today may be different from what you have become accustomed to in the past.

2. Conscientiously face the question of whether this really is God's will, or something you yourself desire.

3. Remember the goodness of God—in the lives of biblical persons, in his promises to us, in the pages of church history, and in your own experience.

4. Ask just what is involved specifically in doing God's will in a particular situation. Be sure that you do precisely that, rather than something less or something you decide to substitute.

5. Ask God for the strength to do his will. If you are not willing to do his will, ask him to make you willing.

6. Remember that the blessings that God will be able to send because of your obedience will continue into the future, perhaps even after your death.

Study Guide

Key Concept Questions

1. Describe three "prerequisites" that the author suggests are necessary for being able to do the will of God.
2. What is one common way in which we can be easily tempted away from genuine obedience in doing the will of God?
3. What are some of the benefits that come to us when we are completely obedient to the will of God?

Bible Investigation

The author makes the assertion that the basic "question" of Christian living is *doing*, not simply *knowing*, the will of God. "The proof of faith is obedience." This truth is dramatically illustrated in the biblical account of Abraham's offer to sacrifice his son Isaac. The importance of "performance" in a believer's life is also emphasized in Hebrews 11, commonly known as "*the* chapter on faith" in the Bible. To enhance your understanding of the connection among faith, obedience, and doing the will of God, look up the Old Testament references that provide the details on the lives of three of the "heroes of faith" mentioned in Hebrews 11: Rahab (Josh. 2; 6:22–25); Barak (Judg. 4–5); Jephthah (Judg. 11–12:7).

What can you conclude about the nature of the faith, obedience, and doing the will of God from these individuals' experiences?

Personal Life Application

Reflect upon a situation in your life in which you felt confident that a chosen course of action was "God's will." Did the accomplishment of your plan run smoothly, or did you encounter some obstacles along the way? How should you view such difficulties? Should you quickly give up on your plans, considering obstacles to be God's attempt to lead in unexpected directions? Or should you work even harder to accomplish your goals, viewing obstacles as Satan's attempt to thwart God's will?

Read Romans 1:8–13 as well as James 4:13–16 to inform your answer.

For Further Thought

In our attempt to obey God and accomplish his will, sometimes we may encounter a moral dilemma in which we must seemingly choose between two equally valid biblical principles. To "obey" one would actually result in "disobeying" the other. What do we do when it appears we must choose the lesser of two evils?

9

Giving to God—
Many Happy Returns?

Malachi 3:6–12

Imagine that you are sitting in church during Sunday morning worship. When the time for the offering comes, you place your envelope in the plate, then resume listening to the music. Before your attention is focused on the music, however, you see something out of the corner of your eye that quickly captures your full attention. Another worshiper, sitting down the pew from you, reaches into the offering plate, grabs a handful of bills, and thrusts them into his pocket.

How would you react? You would be incensed, most likely. How could someone be so insensitive, so greedy, so sacrilegious as to take money that has been given to God? That is stealing from God. It is eternal embezzlement. Your sense of justice would be outraged.

Think about how God must feel when someone steals from him. What does it do to his heart? Now you are prepared to understand his displeasure with those who fail to give him his tithe. In the sight of God, according to Malachi 3:6–12, failure to give the tithe is actually stealing from God. The person who fails to put money in the offering plate is just as much a thief as the person who takes it out. The only difference is that the second person's action is more obvious.

Let's look at the background of the verses in Malachi 3. The people of Israel sinned in many ways. One of these was through failing to give their tithes to God. Because of this, they had failed to receive his blessing. In the imagery Malachi used, the floodgates of heaven are the portals through which God pours out his blessing. Because of their disobedience, he had closed those floodgates to the Israelites. Their crops were not prospering. When their plants bore fruit, devouring locusts took that fruit. But if they would obey God's command, he said he would open the windows of heaven and pour out an abundant, overwhelming blessing. It was not that this one command had a unique connection with God's blessing. Rather, this was apparently the one area that they had particularly neglected, and they especially needed to apply themselves to it.

What about this ancient command to give to the Lord one-tenth of our income? Does it still apply today? And if so, is it realistic? In this day of rising costs, high taxes, and pressures for social conformity, is it really possible for Christians to do the same as the ancient Hebrews? Aren't we freed from keeping the old covenant laws? God expects us to obey this command today, and as with all of his other commands, he will make it possible for us to fulfill it if we follow certain steps.

How Does the Command Still Apply?

We must first recognize the applicability of the command. Jehovah found it necessary to remind the Jews of this. Malachi 3 was, of course, part of their law. But even before the law, the command went back at least as far as Abraham, who paid tithes to Melchizedek, the priest of Jehovah. It appears that this command was always part of God's plan and pattern for the relationship between him and his followers. But we live in a different age than these Jews, a different era in God's plan and dealing with his people. We are no longer under law. Surely under the grace of Jesus Christ we no longer need to practice this ancient rule, do we?

We have already noted that the practice of tithing preceded God's formal introduction of the Mosaic law. Beyond that, we need to take a closer look at Jesus' treatment of the law. He indicated that he had fulfilled the law, and therefore the ceremonial aspects of the law, such as offering sacrifices had terminated. Nonetheless, he said he had not come to destroy the law. At no point did Jesus set aside the practice and fulfillment of the moral law. Nor did he lower the standards or relax its demands. Instead he elevated them. He reminded his hearers that the law told people long ago, "Do not murder." He did not say, however, "You are now under grace; it is all right to kill." He said, "Anyone who is angry with his brother will be subject to judgment" (Matt. 5:21–22). Similarly, the law said, "Do not commit adultery." Jesus said, "Anyone who looks at a woman lustfully has already committed adultery with her in his heart" (5:27–28). He always raised the standard rather than lowered it. Jesus would see the tithe in the same light. He did not speak against it. In fact he commended men for tithing, rebuking them only for neglecting the other matters of spiritual responsibility (23:23).

Some people see 1 Corinthians 16:2 as a suggestion that God expects the tithe from some, while others whom he has prospered to a lesser extent would give less. This is the principle of "proportionate giving." If what we have noted above is correct, then there is another possible interpretation that is probably preferable: The tithe is the minimum expected of all; but there are some whom God has especially prospered, who ought to give more than this.

We may find ourselves asking, "But why should I give 10 percent of my money to God?" This is an important question, but it is improperly phrased. It is like the question, "Have you stopped beating your wife?" These questions indicate that we have gone wrong on a fundamental concept, right at the start. It is really not our money. The Bible teaches that everything in this world is God's (Ps. 50:9–10). The money belongs to him, and he has placed it with us to use in accomplishing his purposes in this world. This is the point of Jesus' stewardship parables (for example, look at Matt. 25:14–30). Our question then is not, "What is the least amount of my money that I must give to God?" Instead it is, "What is the least of God's money that I need to keep for myself?"

Malachi used strong words in reporting God's message: "You are *robbing* me." The Hebrews were engaged in what could be called eternal embezzlement, stealing from God. What they were keeping for themselves was not theirs, but God's.

A Promise for the Obedient

We need to remember the promise given for faithful obedience to this command. Jehovah did not ask for blind obedience from the people. He invited them to put him to a test. They were to bring all the tithes into the storehouse, into his house, and he promised that when they did this he would pour upon them a blessing so great they would be unable to contain it. They could assess for themselves whether he was faithful.

What was the nature of this blessing? Was it material? Certainly in part this was the case. God would again bless their farming endeavors. But that was not the major part. God has never promised to make all of his children wealthy, although he does entrust some believers with unusual amounts of material possessions. He has promised, however, to provide all of our needs. Some of us can bear abundant testimony to this. Whenever I mention this in a sermon, there are always numerous people who come to me afterwards and tell me how God has provided in their lives. Let me share one personal experience.

Near the end of my junior year at the University of Minnesota, I saw a financial crisis developing. My small reserves were almost exhausted. I had a night job at a funeral home, which enabled me to study on the job. I wanted to keep it, but it did not pay enough to meet my anticipated needs, even with adding a full-time summer job. I could not expect any help from home. Each of us four children received $50 when we graduated from high school. That is all that our parents could afford to give.

As I thought about my situation, there seemed to be three possibilities: a scholarship, a Christmas job at the post office, or an additional part-time job. I had seen advertisements for part-time jobs on the 6:00–10:00 A.M. shift at the newspaper in Minneapolis, and I knew that during the winter and spring quarters I would have no classes before 10:30 A.M. I applied for a scholarship.

When I returned in the fall I was told that my application was still being actively considered. I applied for a Christmas position at the Minneapolis post office at the earliest possible date. And then I waited as the fall quarter went on. I heard nothing from the Bureau of Student Loans and Scholarships; I heard nothing from the post office. I began to get anxious. Then one dark day in early December I saw a small article in the newspaper that said that several thousand temporary employees had been sworn in to work at the post office during the Christmas rush. It appeared that I had been left out. Even though I was quickly running out of money, I knew the promise in Malachi 3 and I claimed it. Someone had taught me to tithe, and I had continued practicing it.

The next day I received a letter instructing me to report to the main post office for swearing in. I finished my fall quarter examinations and then worked seventeen hours and ten minutes the first day. When I arrived home at

2:00 A.M., weary but happy, there was one letter on my desk. The return address on the long envelope said, "Bureau of Student Loans and Scholarships, University of Minnesota." I ripped it open and read the first line: "I am pleased to inform you that you have been awarded a Nash Foundation Scholarship in the amount of $200." I was rich! Then on the last day of December I went to the Minneapolis *Star and Tribune* and inquired about an early morning job. The personnel director told me that there were no openings just then, but that I could complete an application if I wished. While I was filling out the form, the head of the display advertising department telephoned the personnel office about a new opening. He interviewed me, gave me the job, and I began the following Monday.

God keeps his promise. He provides for our needs when we keep his command. Sometimes we glibly claim Paul's promise, "And my God will meet all your needs according to his glorious riches in Christ Jesus" (Phil. 4:19). But we forget that Paul wrote this to the Philippians, the only church that was faithful in supporting his work with their gifts. The promise was only to them and to those who follow their example.

The primary blessing for tithing is spiritual. When we keep this commandment, we have the satisfaction of knowing we have done God's will. We can face God squarely. We can pray confidently, knowing that we are not neglecting his instructions to us. And he grants us success in our service because nothing (in this area, at least) stands as an obstruction to his using us. We are able in all these areas to say, "I have done what you have asked, O Lord."

God Asks You to Test Him

When we understand and accept the truth in any area of the Christian life, we still will come to a point of decision. We must recognize this truth as being as important as any obligation we have and give it high priority. We must resolve to obey.

For people who are not now practicing tithing, to begin may seem like a gigantic step. Yet it is a matter of saying, "I will do this, I will give the first tenth of my income, and then I will budget around it, making whatever adjustments are necessary in my lifestyle." If tomorrow you were presented with a 10 percent reduction in pay and you had no other option but to continue in your present position, you would find a way to get along.

In my pastorate in Minneapolis I met a couple who had found the truth of this. They had been married several years and had acquired a modest but comfortable home. They realized one day that they had been neglecting tithing. They resolved that they would begin tithing again, and would make whatever adjustments were necessary, even to the point of selling their lovely home and moving into a more modest house. Because the husband was a real estate salesman whose income fluctuated, their decision was a particularly bold one. God honored that couple's decision. The man's real estate sales increased, and they did not have to give up their home. I am sure that they will always be tithers.

For some people, tithing may mean beginning by making a start. While that may sound redundant, it carries a special meaning. Some people are so committed to installment payments that it is very difficult to move all the way to giving 10 percent. And they may not have sufficient faith to make that big a leap all at once. The Lord honors the honest resolve to do his will completely, coupled with a small but concrete step in that direction. Perhaps you are now giving about 2 percent and can move to 4 percent. Then, as some debts are retired (and not replaced with others), you can move to 6, 8, and eventually 10 percent, and more. God enables the person who is honestly trying to fulfill his will.

What God asks is that we put him to that test. If we do, he will prove his ability to enable us to keep his command. The test involves giving him a thorough and sustained opportunity to demonstrate what he will do. Sometimes a church will have a "tithing Sunday," on which all are asked to give one-tenth of their income from the previous week. This indicates the giving potential of the church (income the following Sunday sometimes drops below the normal Sunday average), but it is not an adequate trial of God's plan. Some people try tithing for a week (or even a month) and find that it doesn't work. That reminds me of a man who heard that feathers make a good pillow, so he got one feather and tried it with disappointing results. Let's give God an adequate opportunity. Quite a number of people have tried tithing on a short-term basis. For the rare individuals who claim to have given tithing a sustained test and found that it did not work, there are literally scores who testify that it does.

Preachers are fond of saying that nine-tenths with the blessing of God is more than ten-tenths without that blessing. As mathematics that makes little sense. But what good is all our income without a job at which to earn it, or the health and strength to perform a job if we have one? We are more dependent upon God's care and provision than we realize. After all has been said, he commands, "Bring!" (Mal. 3:10).

This command applies to us, as it did to the ancient Hebrews. Remember the promise that God has given and resolve to obey his command. Then God will open the floodgates of heaven and pour out his overflowing blessing upon you too.

Put It into Practice

Tithing will be easier if we:

1. Recognize that everything we have and are is God's, not ours. He has simply lent it to us for his use. Re-read passages such as Psalm 50 and Matthew 25:14–30.

DOES IT MATTER HOW I LIVE?

2. Remember God's promise for faithful obedience to this command, and bear in mind that God is faithful and his promises cannot fail (Heb. 6:18). Observe people in Scripture, such as Joseph and Paul, who found that God kept his promises. Consult your own experience and the testimony of others about his faithful care and provision for those who place their trust in him.

3. Study carefully your wants and seek to determine the bare minimum of your actual needs. Take one-tenth of your income and make it the first priority in your spending. If you cannot immediately move to 10 percent, make a beginning and then retire some of your indebtedness, resolving not to get similarly committed. Meanwhile, make another step toward a full tithe. As opportunities come, give to God over and above the tithe.

4. Give God an adequate opportunity to prove his faithfulness. Practice tithing over a prolonged period of time. Keep note of his blessings, concentrating primarily upon spiritual and relationship aspects. Share these blessings with others, and listen to and profit from their testimonies of blessing.

Study Guide

Key Concept Questions

1. What does the author believe to be Jesus' viewpoint on the issue of tithing? What reasons does he give to support this position?
2. What is the primary blessing that Christians can expect from God when they are faithful in their giving?
3. What should we actually do to "test" God in the area of tithing?

Bible Investigation

When contemplating "testing" God in the area of giving as suggested in Malachi 3:8–12, it could become very tempting to become motivated to give simply in order to get something good from God in return. Read the entire Book of Malachi. Besides robbing God of the tithe, what else were the people doing or not doing that God condemned? Would the restoring of the tithe have been enough to correct this situation? Is it likely then that the promise of God's blessing would have been attached *only* to obedience in giving? What conclusion can you make regarding the relationship among obedience to God in all areas of our lives, obedience to God in our giving, *and* the granting of his blessing?

Personal Life Application

Scripture teaches us that a believer's inner disposition to what God commands him or her to do is very important. Most Christians seem to know "in their heads" that "God loves a cheerful giver," yet in reality a "reluctant, grudging heart" prevents them from being faithful in giving.

Examine your own attitudes toward giving as well as your own personal giving patterns. Which viewpoint does your actual practice of giving reflect—that giving is a rather difficult and burdensome requirement, or that giving is

DOES IT MATTER HOW I LIVE?

actually a privilege that brings with it a special kind of joy? Which specific scriptural principles have guided you in your giving? If you have resisted the idea of giving a tithe, determine what has prevented you from doing so.

Carefully read 2 Corinthians 8–9. From this passage, identify principles to be applied to the act of giving as well as insights into the nature of the giver. Also note David's understanding of the act of giving in 1 Chronicles 21:18–28.

For Further Thought

Many Christians today believe that the Old Testament pattern of tithing is no longer operational. These Christians agree with the author's claim that Jesus' fulfilling of the Old Testament law eliminated the need to follow certain of its ceremonial aspects. Since they see tithing as one of these "legal" requirements, they have decided that it is no longer binding for Christians today. The author presents scriptural evidence to the contrary. He suggests that tithing fits under the category of God's "moral" law, which Christ in no way abolished but instead reinforced and "elevated."

Read Jesus' condemnations of the Pharisees in Matthew 23 (esp. v. 23) and Luke 11:37–54 (esp. v. 42). How should the practice of tithing be viewed, according to these passages? If it's true that tithing should not be "neglected" or "left undone," does that not make it a required obligation for a Christian today? In light of this understanding, how should we interpret 2 Corinthians 9:7?

10

How to Share Your Faith—
Without the Butterflies

John 4:1–30

In the city of Minneapolis, a pastor conducted a course in personal evangelism. During the weeks of the course he emphasized the importance of prayer support for evangelism. For each team of two who went out to make evangelistic calls on any given night, a corresponding team of two people remained at the church to pray for them. When the training course ended and the first night of calling was to begin, thirty-two people volunteered to stay at the church and pray—and only two volunteered to go out calling. For all the doorbells I have rung, I must admit that when I make this kind of call a little voice within me still says, "I hope they're not home!"

One of the most frightening ideas to many Christians is that of trying to witness to an unsaved person and invite that person to accept Christ. The problem is not merely that we lack knowledge about techniques. There are abundant courses, books, and other materials available for learning the how-to of personal evangelism. Yet more is involved than technique. God's enabling is necessary. The grace of God will make us useful witnesses if we note and practice several basics. There is no better illustration and example of this than our Lord gave us. In John 4:1–30 we see him dealing with a lost person on a one-to-one basis. From this passage we can learn how to engage in personal evangelism.

Keep Your Eyes Open

The first factor is alertness to an opportunity. Jesus and the disciples were traveling through Samaria. It was mid-day and the disciples had gone into the village to get provisions. Jesus remained at Jacob's well to rest. As he sat there, a woman from the village came to draw water. In everyday language we'd say that she "happened to come along." But that isn't how Jesus saw it. Because he knew God was at work in all things, he recognized there was a reason why he was there at the same time as she. It was an opportunity for him to speak to someone in need about the redeeming grace that he had brought. So he initiated a conversation with her.

There were plenty of reasons why Jesus could have remained silent. He was off-duty. He was tired and needed to rest. Besides this, it would not be good public relations to be seen talking to this woman. In the first place, she was Samaritan, and there was a deep animosity between the Samaritans and the Jews going all the way back to the return from captivity. The Jews and Samaritans ordinarily avoided any dealings with one another (John 4:9). Jesus and the disciples usually avoided traveling through Samaria in their journeys between Judea and Galilee, crossing over instead into Perea, and spending an additional day en route. On one occasion, when his opponents were particularly abusive, they accused Jesus of being a Samaritan and demon-possessed (8:48). (It is difficult to know which charge was considered more serious.) To be seen talking to a Samaritan would not build the disciples' confidence in him. Further, she was a sinful woman, and association with her would not help his rapport with either the disciples or the local Samaritans. Yet Jesus shared his message with her because she had a need, and he knew that God had brought them to the same place at the same time.

We have a tendency to "program" evangelism—to set up times, places, and techniques for telling people about Christ. These programs are important and can be very effective. But some of the finest opportunities are not deliberately planned or scheduled. We will recognize them if we are sufficiently alert and sensitive to detect them.

I have a Christian friend in the Chicago area who found himself paired up in a goose blind with the president of one of the largest breweries in the United States, because his hunting partner was ill. The hunting was slow, and their conversation turned to various subjects, including world conditions. The other man commented that he was glad his children were grown, because he would hate to try to rear young people in today's world. My friend, who at the time had four teenagers, commented that as Christians he and his wife had committed their children to the Lord, and were trusting him to enable them to rear them the right way. He told the man about what Christ meant to him in his personal life. He did not convert the brewer that day, but when they parted the other man said, "Please let me know the next time you are going hunting down here. I'd like to hunt with you again." There is no way my friend could have made an appointment to present Christ to that executive, but the Lord put the two of them in the goose blind together for reasons other than goose hunting.

When my friend told me this incident, I thought about all the time I had spent in restaurant booths and plane seats with other Christians. One day about two weeks after he told me this story, I went out to play golf. None of my usual partners were available—none of them! So I went to the golf course by myself. As I approached the first tee, another man came from a different direction. Simultaneously we asked, "Playing alone?" We introduced ourselves and off we went together. We both had the same problem with our game, so we spent a lot of time walking together down the right side of the fairway. He was a talkative salesman who had achieved his quota early and was celebrating. About the ninth or tenth hole he brought up the subject of "religion," as he called it, and about two holes later I had an opportunity to tell him what Christ meant to me. I realized that, instead of playing golf with other Christian professors, perhaps I should just go out to the golf course and see whom the Lord had put there for me to meet. Alertness to the opportunity is the first essential factor of personal evangelism.

The Lost Truly Are Lost

The second factor in Jesus' dealing with the Samaritan woman was his awareness of her true condition. Many distracting factors about this woman's situation might have turned Jesus away from her real need, which was for living water. The first was her social problem. She had had five husbands and was now living with a man to whom she was not married. Whether she had been widowed this many times, or divorced, we do not know, but certainly her present situation was not right. Jesus could have said, "Get this twisted social situation straightened out, and everything will be all right." But he did not. Or, he could have been distracted by her "church problem." Her fathers worshiped in a place in Samaria. The true worship of Jehovah was carried on in Jerusalem. How could she properly relate to God if she was involved with the wrong religious group? Again, Jesus did not allow himself to be distracted by a secondary issue. He stuck to the central problem. As important as these matters were, the most significant fact was that she was a sinner. All temporal means of satisfaction could be only that—temporary. She needed the living water that Jesus alone could give.

This woman's need was apparent. Jesus could detect her condition. Even the time of day that she came to the well may have indicated her sinfulness. Because of the kind of life she was living, she went at noon when none of the other women would be there, so she would not be exposed to their taunts. Many of the people Jesus encountered were not such obvious sinners. For instance, Nicodemus—religious, moral, educated, sophisticated—came to Jesus at night on one occasion. Certainly he had not committed the grosser sort of sins that this unnamed woman was guilty of. But Jesus said to him, and to the rest of the religious officials of that day, "You [plural] must be born again" (3:7). Whether religious or not, cultured or not, a sinner is a sinner and must be dealt with as such. Some of the people we meet will not have obvious sins. Some of them will be ethical, cultured, thoughtful, kindly, genteel, and even religious. Yet they are in need of the living water found only in Jesus Christ.

In our dealings with other people, we need to be aware of their spiritual condition. The fundamental fact is that all people, apart from having accepted Jesus Christ in an act of saving faith, are sinners and consequently separated from God. We may see many distracting features, some of which are symptoms of this fundamental fact. But we must keep this basic reality firmly in mind. Secondary problems are indeed secondary. Sometimes, of course, we will need to deal with these problems before the spiritual problem, or simultaneously with it. People who are physically hungry will not be able to think clearly about their spiritual needs. Nonetheless, in helping them meet these very basic needs, we should not lose sight of the primary goal of introducing them to Jesus Christ.

Once I went to a doctor about a persistent throat infection that was making me hoarse. Early in our conversation the doctor noticed my bad case of dandruff, which he tactfully pointed out could be a problem for someone in my occupation, where appearance is quite important. He wrote a prescription for a shampoo that would take care of it. As he was about to terminate our conversation by excusing himself, I said, "But, Doctor—my throat!" I appreciated his concern for my dandruff problem, but in dealing with it he had overlooked the more important problem. Evangelism does not consist of straightening out people's social maladjustments or getting them to the right church. It is a matter of bringing people to the source of the living water, the forgiveness of sins.

Get Down to Business

The third essential in personal evangelism is applying the gospel. Jesus might have written off the possibility of this woman being transformed, because of the extent of her depravity. But he knew that the living water would suffice for anyone, including her. He could have been repulsed by her sinfulness. He was the perfectly sinless one, and the type of life she was living was in direct contradiction to his perfect nature. But Jesus did not pull away from her, because he had come into the world to save sinners, not to condemn them.

Jesus did not allow himself to be deterred from his tasks either consciously or unconsciously. The Samaritan woman raised her deflectors to protect herself against the message that he presented. She tried to get him off into a debate about which was the correct place to worship (4:20). She flattered him, (4:19), hoping that he would become self-concerned and forget about what he was telling her. Nonetheless, Jesus consistently shared his message. Gently but persistently he told her that there was a source of satisfaction, which unlike the water she was drawing from the well, and the various activities and people in her life, would give her permanent satisfaction. He knew that there was only one solution to her problem, and that it was in him. He knew that the message he bore was true, and that it would work. This came to a focus in his statement, "I who speak to you am he" (v. 26).

In our experiences with evangelism there will be people whom we may not like. Consequently, we may not especially want to bring them the gospel. There will be people who by the depth of their sinfulness will incline us to despair. We may wonder if God can save them. But there is no one who is beyond the grace of God. There is no evidence in the Book of Acts that the early church prayed for the salvation of Saul of Tarsus. Indeed, they were skeptical about his reported conversion. If anything, they were probably praying that God would strike him down, take him away. Yet God converted him and made of him one of the greatest apostles. The message of John 4:1–30 is that there is grace for that teenager at the locker next to ours at school, that man at the machine or desk next to ours at work, the housewife in the yard behind ours, the woman at the word processor next to ours. Our task is simply to present the message: "Believe in the Lord Jesus, and you will be saved" (Acts 16:31).

The confidence that we have in this message will determine our boldness in presenting it, and the likelihood that we will do so consistently. And the confidence that it will work for others will in turn be proportional to the extent that we are currently experiencing its reality, satisfaction, and sufficiency in our own lives. One of the keys to being a witness is keeping our own Christian life vital.

As a schoolboy I had few sources of income. Allowances were unknown in our family and part-time employment nonexistent. I had to engage in sales of some type. One year I sold salve for a quarter per can. I pedaled my bicycle from farm to farm selling my salve. The next year I had a problem. I could not sell salve; virtually everyone still had more salve than they needed. I had to find a new prod uct. My best friend had been wiser. He sold garden seeds and now had repeat customers.

I became the local representative for a wonderful product called "The Magic Polishing Cloth." It had polish within the flannel, and was just the thing for polishing metal objects such as silverware. I began selling it and was doing well. Then my brother came home on furlough, and I attempted to sell him a Magic Polishing Cloth. An air force officer, I reasoned, needed to look his best, and my polishing cloth was just the thing he needed to shine his silver bars, wings, and other insignia. But he opened his duffel bag and pulled out something called a "Blitz Cloth," proceeding to demonstrate its qualities. Our mother's silverware had never shined so brightly. My career as a salesman of Magic Polishing Cloths was ended, for I knew now that a vastly superior product existed—one which, unfortunately, I could not sell! I lost confidence.

To keep our confidence we need to be living our Christian lives daily, experiencing the reality of God's present grace, worshiping God, studying his Word, and fellowshiping with his people. Then we will be moved to apply the gospel to the lives of unbelievers.

When Jesus' disciples returned and offered him food he said, "I have food to eat that you know nothing about . . . My food is to do the will of him who sent me" (John 4:31–34). Like Jesus we find satisfaction in helping others receive the redeeming grace of God. In this case, not only did the Samaritan woman believe, but as she told others from her city, they came out to hear Jesus, and many came to believe (vv. 28–30, 39–42).

I was serving as interim pastor of a church in Chicago. The youth decided to put on a Bible school during the spring school vacation (which did not come at Easter). It was to be entirely for neighborhood children who did not attend our church or Sunday school. The teens handled it all themselves. They staffed the school. They went out calling and invited children. They raised the money for materials. Sixty-five children attended and thirteen came to personal faith in Jesus. During the Sunday evening service, the teens shared their experiences with the rest of the church. One by one, as they came to the platform, each told of the joy of leading someone to Christ. Their feet were about twelve inches off the floor. They had found the truth of Jesus' words. Each of us, if we are alert to the opportunities, aware of the need, and apply the gospel, will also find this joy and satisfaction of doing the Father's will.

Put It into Practice

In order to be able to give your personal witness to others, you should:

1. Be alert to possibilities that the Lord has placed a particular person in your path so that you will witness to him or her. Consider especially situations that seem to be disappointments or changes in your plans.

2. Study regularly the passages in the Bible that describe the human predicament, such as Psalm 51, Jeremiah 17, and Romans 3, so that you will see and evaluate people as God does. Note that even such an outwardly moral and religious person as Nicodemus was told by Jesus, "You must be born again" (John 3:7).

3. Practice daily the reality of the Christian life, so that you have something genuine to share with those with whom you speak.

4. Avoid being distracted by things that people bring up that could throw you off the subject. Especially, do not get drawn into arguments or discussions of secondary matters.

5. Pray God will bring you into contact with people who are open to the gospel, to guide you in what you say, and to apply your words of witness and bring about the true work of conversion.

Study Guide

Key Concept Questions

1. The Christian's primary goal in day-to-day dealings with unbelievers, whether in scheduled or incidental encounters, should always be to present Christ. Do you agree or disagree? Why or why not?
2. To be effective in personal evangelism, what three important factors do we need to keep in mind?
3. What determines the degree of boldness with which a believer will present the gospel message?

Bible Investigation

Perhaps part of the reason why some Christians remain oblivious to opportunities to share their faith in Christ is because they haven't acquired a wartime mentality that sees life as an ongoing battle with "the powers of this dark world" for the souls of humankind (Eph. 6:12). Consequently, they don't see the urgency in aggressively "rescuing" those held captive, and they stay far back from the "front lines" of evangelism. In marked contrast to this indifference, the apostle Paul risked his life and suffered greatly in order to "win some." Read 2 Corinthians 5:11–21 to discover four reasons why he remained so strongly motivated to share the gospel: (1) v. 11; (2) vv. 14–15; (3) vv. 16–17; (4) vv. 19–20.

Certainly these same factors should stimulate us toward active evangelism, as should Jesus' own example. Read the story of Jesus' encounter with Zacchaeus in Luke 19:1–10. Why did Luke report this event (see especially v. 10)? How should apprehending Jesus' mission on earth influence our understanding of our own mission here on earth?

Personal Life Application

Consider the following scenario. You have developed an "over-the-fence" friendship with a new neighbor who one day rather suddenly reveals to you that his life is "in shambles." His marriage is on shaky ground, he suspects his teenage daughter is sexually involved with an immature high school drop-out, and now his job has been placed in jeopardy. How will you respond to this person's needs? Plan a strategy that will include presenting the gospel message.

For Further Thought

Some well-intentioned Christians refrain from ever taking the initiative in talking about Christ with an unbeliever because they suppose that when the time is right, God will spontaneously nudge them and clearly give them the right words to say. To these individuals, to prepare and "rehearse" a testimony in advance could actually inhibit the work of the Holy Spirit in the process of evangelism. Contrast Luke 12:11–12 with 1 Peter 3:15 and 2 Timothy 4:2 in order to gain insight into this belief. Carefully note the context of each passage. In what kind of situation is there a promise that the Holy Spirit will "teach you what you should say"? In general, should we expect to effectively share our faith with comfort and at our convenience? See 1 Corinthians 15:58; Colossians 1:28–29; 2:1.

11

God's Cure for Discouraged Hearts

Psalms 42–43

Several years ago I heard a man say that for five years he had read one book per week and a biography each month. That meant that in five years he had read sixty biographies. There was only one of those sixty famous men and women he read about whose biography did not mention that he or she had been discouraged at some point in life. But even though the biographer did not write anything about this one man being discouraged, that does not mean that he was never discouraged.

Biographies that get published are not written about ordinary people. They are written about unusual people, outstanding people, accomplished people. And even among these individuals, discouragement at one point or another is virtually universal. So it is surprising to find a person who breaks the pattern.

You are probably wondering who that one individual was, of whom the biographer did not think it significant enough to mention that he had been discouraged. It was

Henry Ford. I bet, however, that Henry was discouraged at least once, and I think I know when.

In Greenfield Village in Dearborn, Michigan, the Ford Motor Company has assembled an outdoor museum. Many significant buildings were brought from their original locations and erected in the park. One is the small brick building in which Henry Ford constructed his first functioning automobile. A portion of one wall has obviously been rebuilt. The board beside the building explains that when Ford completed that first mechanical wonder and it came time to take it out for a test run, he discovered that it was too large to fit through the door! So he broke out the wall, pushed the car out, and later rebuilt the wall. Did Ford, when he discovered what he had done, just for a fleeting moment feel a bit of discouragement? I think so. If he did not, his exception simply accentuates the rule: Discouragement is a part of life.

If discouragement comes to all humans, Christians are not immune. We are exposed to the same types of circumstances and problems as all other people. The uniqueness of the Christian experience does not totally shelter us from difficult experiences. Yet we do have unusual resources with which to cope with the problems. In Psalms 42 and 43, we read the personal testimony of a saint as he faced a situation that was bringing him discouragement. We see, too, how he grasped the means that God had provided for dealing with such situations. And since these psalms are not a dry discourse upon the subject, but an expression of personal experience, they convey a note of reality, of authenticity. Something within us naturally responds. We, too, will encounter discouraging situations, but God has provided several means with which we can overcome these circumstances, if we know how to draw upon his provision.

Find the Cause

The first step in overcoming discouragement is to discover the cause. The psalmist searched his own soul and repeatedly asked himself, "Why are you downcast, O my soul? Why so disturbed within me?" (Ps. 42:5, 11; 43:5). This was more than just a rhetorical question in which he asked himself, "Why are you, why should you be, cast down?" (i.e., "You have no reason to be discouraged"). There were reasons for his depression, and the psalmist sought to determine these so that he could deal with them. He progressed beyond his general self-inquiry to indicate that the problem was, at least in part, caused by the oppression of the enemy (Pss. 42:9–10; 43:2). Beyond that, he asked why God failed to vindicate him. He sought to get to the bottom of the difficulty.

We need to ask this question when discouragement comes. Sometimes the cause of our reaction will be evident. At other times we will have to ask both ourselves and God why a certain situation is present, or why we react as we do. There are a number of reasons why discouragement comes. The following list suggests a few.

Discouragement may come because we have *a wrong relationship to God*. Humans are made for the purpose of fellowship with God. When we fulfill that purpose, we find life satisfying. When we are not in that intended relationship, life is difficult—and it ought to be. It is like trying to live life in a way it was never intended to be lived. Jesus told Saul of Tarsus, "It is hard for you to kick against the goads" (Acts 26:14). This is also true of a person who has initially entered into the relationship (become a Christian) but has deviated from it. Thus after his sin, David prayed, "Restore to me the joy of your salvation" (Ps. 51:12). He had not lost his salvation, but he had lost the joy of it because sin interfered with his proper relationship to God. Living out of fellowship with God is like trying to walk backwards. It can be done, but it is very unnatural. Our bodies are not designed or assembled in a way that makes this a practical way to function. It is much easier to walk in harmony with the way we are built.

We may also become discouraged because we have *an improper self-valuation.* We may err in this in either direction. We may have too high an opinion of ourselves. In Romans 12:3 Paul indicates the importance of not thinking of ourselves more highly than we ought to think, but rather to think soberly. Each year there are college freshmen who pack at the end of the first term and go home, not to return to school again. They have discovered that they are not college material. Each spring aspiring baseball rookies are "cut," told that they must return to the minors, because they are not ready for the major leagues. It is no disgrace to find that we are not suited for something that we have aspired to. It is God who causes one person to differ from another. Paul points this out in Romans 12:3–8. We need to learn about ourselves and not frustrate ourselves by trying to be or do what God did not intend for us.

The opposite error is failure to recognize or be or do all that we can. Thus, Paul urged Timothy to rekindle the gift that was within him through the laying on of Paul's hands (2 Tim. 1:6). If we fail to realize or to achieve our full, God-given potential, we will experience frustration, boredom, and restlessness.

We may also experience discouragement because we fail to see life's events in their proper proportion. Sometimes the events of the moment overwhelm us because they are so close that they blot out other important realities. Yet the believer judges life's individual events in the light of all of eternity. Paul says, "I consider that our present sufferings are not worth comparing with glory that will be revealed in us" (Rom. 8:18). Here is a thought-experiment for you: Look at today's date on the calendar, then ask yourself what was troubling or discouraging you on this day one year ago, two years ago, five years ago. Unless there was something very unusual about the date, or you have an extraordinary memory, it is unlikely that you can recall. We should ask, as Christians: How important will this be to me ten years, a hundred years, a thousand years from now? Whatever the cause of our discouragement, we will seek to discover it through self-examination, through prayer for the Spirit to give us understanding, through the counsel of godly friends. Sometimes in more serious cases of discouragement, this will mean seeking professional counseling help. The psalmist prayed, "Search me, O God, and know my heart; test me and know my anxious thoughts. See if there is any offensive way in me, and lead me in the way everlasting" (Ps. 139:23–24).

Developing God-Based Optimism

The second step in overcoming discouragement with God's help is to develop an optimistic attitude. This is not a humanistic positive-thinking approach, but a biblical mind-set that always takes God into account in our interpretation of events. An event and its interpretation are two different things.

The events of life are like a pane of glass in a window. You sit in your living room looking out the window. You can focus your eyes on the surface of the glass itself. If so, you will simply see reflections of yourself, others in the room, and the furniture. Or you can look through the glass, focusing your eyes on the objects outdoors. Then you will see the reality beyond your own room. We may choose either to look at the events themselves, or we may look through the events—beyond them—to the reality of God at work in and through the events of life. This was Joseph's understanding when he spoke to his brothers about their act of selling him into slavery in Egypt: "You intended to harm me, but God intended it for good" (Gen. 50:20). Where we focus our attention is a matter of our own choice. It will determine our state of mind.

In Psalms 42 and 43 the psalmist recalls the goodness and greatness of God, and dwells upon it. He remembers what God has done and been and meant to him in the past: "These things I remember as I pour out my soul: how I used to go with the multitude, leading the procession to the house of God, with shouts of joy and thanksgiving among the festive throng" (Ps. 42:4). He dwells upon sources of encouragement. Doing this will bring a change in mood and state of mind.

There is a significant difference between a pessimist and an optimist. An optimist believes that this is the best of all possible worlds; a pessimist is afraid he is right. An optimist looks at a glass of water and says, "It is half full." A pessimist looks at the same glass and says, "It is half empty." An optimist says, "Every gray cloud has a silver lining"; a pessimist says, "But don't forget every silver lining has a gray cloud." In each case, the two have the same data available to them. The difference is in what they emphasize.

Paul, in Philippians 4, wrote from a prison cell: "Rejoice in the Lord always. I will say it again: Rejoice! . . . And the peace of God, which transcends all understanding, will guard your hearts and your minds in Christ Jesus" (4, 7). This sounds like good advice, but it is easier to give advice than to practice it. In the verses that immediately follow, Paul tells us how to do it: "Finally, brothers, whatever is true, whatever is noble, whatever is right, whatever is pure, whatever is lovely, whatever is admirable—if anything is excellent or praiseworthy—think about such things. Whatever you have learned or received or heard from me, or seen in me—put it into practice. And the God of peace will be with you" (vv. 8–9). That's the key—what we concentrate on. Think on ugly, painful things and you'll be discouraged. Think on the reality and promises of God and you will be encouraged.

Sometimes our problem is that we take ourselves too seriously, and don't take God seriously enough. We sin or fail and we get down on ourselves. When people tell me, "I let God down," I am tempted to ask, "How long have you been holding him up?" Here is another experiment: Stick your finger in a glass of water, then pull it out and see how large a hole it leaves. The point is this: With or without us, the natural laws of God keep functioning. Although God is disappointed when we fail him, he is not overcome by it. He is almighty and his strength is great enough to overcome our failures.

Depend upon a Powerful, Loving God

A third way to overcome discouragement is to depend upon God. The psalmist said, "Put your hope in God, for I will yet praise him, my Savior and my God" (Ps. 42:5, 11; 43:5). He not only thought about God; he placed his trust in him. This was ultimately his basis for confidence in the face of discouraging circumstances.

Trouble has a way of revealing our real attitude toward God. When trouble comes it either draws a person closer to God, in dependence upon him, or it embitters the person. Some react by avoiding God. They do not attend church, read the Bible, or pray. If you had a friend and you refused to visit her, talk to her on the telephone, or read her letters, it would be safe to say that you were angry with her. If we react that way to God, it is likely that we resent him or blame him for the problems that come to us. Other people will draw closer to God in time of need, reasoning that their need for him is greater than ever.

While serving as a student assistant pastor, I visited two hospital patients. Both were in the same hospital, both had terminal cancer, and both knew their condition. The first was a retired man who had lived a full life, and whose family was largely grown. When I entered his room I could feel the smoldering resentment. He blamed God for his condition. The other patient was a housewife in her early thirties, with a husband and young children who needed her. When I entered her room, it was like walking into a place filled with sunshine. She talked about what the Lord meant to her in her situation. Often she said something like, "If ever I needed the Lord, I need him now." I don't know whether my visits helped her, but I always left that room buoyed up by what I experienced there. And I always called on her *after* I called on the man. Trusting God for his solution to our depressing circumstances will be the basis for our hope and for overcoming discouragement.

We will not always be able to understand or explain discouraging events and circumstances to ourselves and to others. Sometimes all we will be able to do is trust, knowing that if we saw it all we would know. But the one thing that we can be sure of is that God is a great and good God and that he loves us, regardless of what the circumstances may be.

A century ago, Charles Haddon Spurgeon, the great Baptist "prince of preachers," preached each Sunday from the pulpit of the Metropolitan Tabernacle in London. Great crowds came to hear him. Yet even in an eminently successful ministry he had discouraging moments. One of these came when he had labored all morning in his study, apparently fruitlessly. He left his study to take a walk. The wind was blowing and he noticed a weathervane, directed by the wind. Suddenly the wind changed direction, and the weathervane turned in response. "Then I understood," said Spurgeon, "that, no matter which way the wind blows, God loves us." We can trust him.

As Christians we experience as many troubles as anyone else, but they need not overcome us. Paul wrote: "We are hard pressed on every side, but not crushed; perplexed, but not in despair; persecuted, but not abandoned; struck down, but not destroyed" (2 Cor. 4:8–9). It can be the same for us. If we discover the cause of our discouragement, develop the right way of viewing life, and depend upon God, then we will experience his cure for discouragement.

DOES IT MATTER HOW I LIVE?

Put It into Practice

To deal with discouragement in your life, you can:

1. Seek to determine the cause, by observing whether something that would produce discouragement is present in your life and whether you are living life the way God intended it to be lived. Ask the indwelling Holy Spirit to show you the cause of your discouragement.

2. Study the passages that tell of the goodness, power, and love of God, especially those in the Book of Psalms. Study passages that promise God's future triumph over sin, such as the Book of Revelation.

3. Recognizing your own insufficiency to cope with many of the threatening circumstances in life, place your trust in God. Realize that you will not always understand fully what God is doing or how he is working. Nevertheless, ask him to take control of this aspect of your life.

4. If the problem of discouragement appears to be serious or prolonged, see a Christian professional counselor, who can help you understand the nature of your problem and how you can help bring your biblical beliefs to bear upon the problem.

Study Guide

Key Concept Questions

1. To what extent is discouragement a normal part of life? Is this as true for Christians as it is for non-Christians? Why or why not?
2. Specifically, what are three steps that the author suggests for drawing upon God's provisions in order to overcome discouragement?
3. Identify some of the root causes of discouragement.
4. What is the difference between "God-based optimism" and a "humanistic positive-thinking approach" for overcoming discouragement?

Bible Investigation

IDEA A

Read the account of Elijah's encounter with the prophets of Baal on Mount Carmel in 1 Kings 18, and the aftermath of this episode in chapter 19. What reasons can you give for Elijah's despondency? In what specific ways did God minister to Elijah? Considering the kind of help that God provided, what do we learn about what it takes to recover from a discouraging setback?

IDEA B

Sometimes dealing with a series of difficult obstacles can eventually give way to real discouragement. Read the account of the rebuilding of the wall of Jerusalem from Nehemiah 4 and 6. Analyze the different kinds of struggles that Nehemiah faced. Despite the opposition, Nehemiah managed to complete this task without becoming discouraged in the process. Identify as many strategies as you can that helped Nehemiah to confidently remain steadfast in his responsibility.

Personal Life Application

To fight discouragement, the author states that we should learn to intentionally focus our attention in ways that can "positively" determine our state of mind. This skill can be practiced and developed in part by learning how to control our emotions in response to negative actions or words. Reflect back on a time when you felt particularly discouraged by what you perceived to be a critical evaluation or rejection by another person. How did you overcome this form of discouragement? What should be our approach toward it? See John 12:43 and Psalm 118:6.

For Further Thought

Feeling controlled and "used" by other people can often result in serious discouragement and even depression in certain individuals who may passively resign themselves to such treatment. Such victims of manipulating by others are sometimes advised to acquire "assertiveness training" in order to learn how to stand up for themselves. Can "assertive" behavior be compatible with a Christlike spirit of humility? Why or why not?

12

How to Live on Daily Rations, and Enjoy It

Matthew 6:25–34

What would you do if you saw someone dressed in a heavy fur coat, cap, gloves, and a ski mask in 100 degree weather? Or someone walking down a street in below freezing weather wearing only a swimsuit? Undoubtedly, you would laugh or shake your head. Wise people adjust their behavior to the circumstances. We do that in other realms besides attire. When driving a car, we slow down in rain, ice, or fog. We are restrained and formal in dignified ceremonies, but relaxed and casual with friends at a party. Making such adjustments is necessary for comfort, and in some cases even for survival.

In addition to our physical and social environment, we operate in a third environment, which in many ways is the most important. Tragically, however, many people are unaware of it because it is unseen, intangible. Christians believe that the supreme truth about the universe is that it has been created and is controlled by an invisible but all-powerful and loving being whom they call "God." Because he is directing the course of history, it is important that we understand his working and relate to it. If we do, we will find that life makes sense and is filled with meaning. If we live contrary to God's will (either ignorantly or intentionally), we will ultimately be disappointed.

This was the problem that Jesus addressed in Matthew 6:25–34—adjusting to God's ways of working. The disciples were anxious about the future: what they would eat, what they would drink, what they would wear. Their concern about tomorrow was destroying their enjoyment of the present and anticipation of the future. Gently but clearly, Jesus diagnosed their problem and suggested the solution: They must understand that God deals out life one day at a time and live in that same day-by-day fashion. "Therefore do not worry about tomorrow," he said, "for tomorrow will worry about itself" (Matt. 6:34). Jesus was not speaking against long-range planning. Nothing in Scripture would support such an interpretation. Indeed, the Christian message seems to urge the ultimate in long-range planning: preparation for eternity. Jesus was seeking to combat long-range worry, anxiety about tomorrow, over which one ultimately has no personal control. Jesus applied this truth in several areas, both through his teaching in this passage and elsewhere, and through the life experiences that he led his disciples into. There are three areas of application of this concept of living day by day.

Living on Daily Provisions

The first is physical provisions. Jesus and his disciples did not have an abundance of physical possessions. On one occasion he said, "Foxes have holes and birds of the air have nests, but the Son of Man has no place to lay his head" (Luke 9:58). They did not always know where their next meal would come from. They had to learn to trust God for the next day's food. This is also implicit in the Lord's Prayer, the model prayer that Jesus gave his disciples. He taught them to pray, "Give us today our daily bread" (Matt. 6:11). Whether this was the prayer at evening for the next day, or the morning prayer for the day then beginning, the meaning is the same: "Give us now the food we need for the day next to be lived." It was not a prayer for the needs of a week or a month removed. It was for very present needs.

It is true that God provides for some Christians far in advance. They have large bank accounts and freezers stocked with an abundant supply of food. Most of us, however, do not have our supplies guaranteed for a long period. We are dependent upon our weekly or monthly paycheck. We have to pray, "Give us today our daily bread." Why does God treat us this way? Does he want to keep us groveling before him? No. In his goodness and wisdom God has two definite reasons for this day-to-day way of providing.

The first is the tendency of many of us to splurge. God in his wisdom knows that if we need next month's material resources next month, it is important that we not have them now. In this regard we can learn a great deal about human beings by observing animals. You simply do not go away on a vacation and tell your dog, "Well, Sport, in the corner of the garage you will find a fourteen-day supply of food and water. Have a good time. We'll see you in two weeks." Dogs do not ration food. You would return at the end of that time to find a very emaciated pet, if indeed he were still alive at all.

But are we any wiser than our dogs? The parents of one teenager carefully saved enough money for four years of college education and had invested the money in U.S. savings bonds. When he graduated from high school, the young man decided he would take a vacation. He found a bank that would cash the bonds for him, and for two glorious weeks he really lived! He flew around the country, stayed in the best hotels, ate sumptuously, bought new clothing whenever he wished. In those two weeks he spent the entire amount. God in his wisdom often withholds tomorrow's resources until tomorrow so we will not spend them today.

There is another reason God provides for us on a daily basis. He knows our tendency toward independence. I confess that the amount of time I spend praying tends to be in direct proportion to the amount of trouble and need I have. I fear that if I had everything I needed for the next six months I might say, "So long, God. I'll see you again in half a year." Prayer is much more than petition. It is also praise, confession, intercession, and thanksgiving. God knows that if we must come to him each day to pray, "Give us this day our daily bread," while we are before him we will remember to engage in the full span of prayer. By supplying our physical needs on this daily basis, he is not only giving us what we know we need, but also supplying what we may not realize we need—strengthened faith.

That is how it was with the nation of Israel. As they traveled in the wilderness, God miraculously fed them by providing manna, a wafer-like substance that they found on the ground each morning. God's command to the people through Moses was clear. Each day they were to gather enough for that day only; they were not to attempt to save any over to the next day. Some people thought they could improve upon God's system. They decided to pick a double amount and sleep late the next morning. But in the morning they found that the manna was rotten, stinking, and inedible. God commanded the people to take a double portion of manna on the day before the Sabbath. On the second day this was as fresh and sweet and nutritious as on the first day. Certainly if God could make "day-before-the-Sabbath" manna on the day before the Sabbath, he could have made it any day of the week. But he did not. Each morning, as the children of Israel gathered the manna anew, the truth was underscored: It is by the hand of Jehovah that we live.

DOES IT MATTER HOW I LIVE?

God Gives Daily Strength

The second area of God's daily provision is strength. Jesus himself grew weary, and his strength was renewed by a break in the routine of responsibility. He made some promises to his disciples that doubtless were difficult to believe: "Anyone who has faith in me will do what I have been doing. He will do even greater things than these" (John 14:12) "You will receive power when the Holy Spirit comes on you" (Acts 1:8). He generalized to all of God's people the promise given to the tribe of Asher: "And your strength will equal your days" (Deut. 33:25).

God is wise in his dealings. Suppose that on Friday we received all our strength for Friday, Saturday, Sunday, and Monday. Think of what we could do on Saturday! We could play 108 holes of golf, clean or paint the entire house, or do any of several huge tasks. But what would happen when Monday came and we returned to our jobs? It is good to receive our strength day by day. Only one day's labor need be done with each day's strength. Sometimes we forget this. We look ahead at all we must do and recognize that we do not now have the strength to do it. So we fret. How much better to realize that each day God will give us the strength we need for that day's labor.

Imagine a young bride standing with her beloved fiancé before the minister, to be "joined in the bonds of holy matrimony." The minister recites the familiar phrases: "Do you take this man to be your lawful wedded husband, to have and to hold from this day forward, for better or for worse, for richer or for poorer, in sickness and health?" As the minister drones on, the bride's mind begins to wander and she thinks about what this pledge means. She realizes that she will wash the dishes after three meals a day for perhaps the next forty years. Being very good at mathematics, she does some quick calculations: an average of four persons per meal, each with one knife, one or two forks, a spoon or two, a plate, glass or cup and saucer, a salad dish, a dessert dish. In her mind she sees a mountain of one million dirty dishes and one million dirty pieces of silverware! If she pictured this when the minister asked, "Do you . . . ?" she would probably reply, "I do not!" and run for the nearest exit. No one can do two million pieces of tableware at one time. Fortunately, no one must. The family will do each meal's dishes after each meal, or at least each day's dishes at the end of the day. Probably they will stack them in the dishwasher and push the button before retiring for the night.

We can see from this illustration how ludicrous it is to borrow trouble from tomorrow. We do not have the strength today to do tomorrow's task. Yet more than once I have found myself counting all the work I had to do in the coming month and wondering how I would ever manage to do it all. Sometimes I finish a day utterly exhausted, that day's store of energy completely depleted. Yet with every night of rest comes strength for the new day's labor.

A word of caution is in order. If the day's strength is to suffice for the day's tasks, it must be used for that labor. If we procrastinate or dissipate our energies on things other than the intended purposes, we may find that only one day's strength is available, but more than one day's responsibilities are upon us. A few years ago I taught in a Christian liberal arts college. The student health service infirmary had twenty-five beds, and during the last week of each semester they were generally all filled—with students who could not stand the stress of accumulated work. Many of these students failed to do their assignments early in the semester.

Sometimes God provides an extraordinary supply of strength for an extraordinary need. All of us can think back upon a time when work, suffering, or sorrow demanded more than we had within us. We say, "I don't know how I did it," and it is true—we didn't do it. God in that moment of need gave us something extra. I think of Samson, that tragic character in the Old Testament. At the end of his life his strength, eyesight, and honor were all gone. The Philistines brought him out for their amusement. So Samson asked a young man to lead him to the pillars that supported the place. He prayed, "Lord, give me strength—just once more." And God supplied the strength he needed to pull down the building, destroying more of the enemies of Jehovah in his death than he had in his life.

God Gives Guidance as We Need It

There is a third area of God's day-by-day working. It is guidance. All of us would like to know what the future holds a month, a year, ten years in advance. Then we could plan our activities. Sometimes, when a decision will affect the whole direction of our future, God makes his will known for a long period. Usually, though, we live on a day-by-day basis.

That is how it was for the disciples. As far as we know, Jesus did not give them long-range instructions. When he talked about ultimate things, they often failed to understand. The psalmist said in Psalm 119:105, "Your word is a lamp to my feet and a light for my path." He was not describing a great floodlight casting its beam far down the pathway. It was a pan of oil with a wick that lighted the path just far enough to see where to take the next step. On a dark night you could not see the place of your tenth, fifth, or even third step. But that was not necessary. You could not take the third or fifth or tenth step until you took the first step. And as you did, the lamp moved forward with you, illuminating the spot where you were to step next.

God guided the people of Israel in their wanderings through the wilderness by a pillar of cloud. While they knew the ultimate destination in general, they did not know the intermediate steps. The guiding cloud moved only a short distance ahead of them. As they followed, obeying the guidance they already had received, the cloud moved on.

The wisdom of God is apparent. Were we to know all the steps in God's plan, we might attempt to take short-cuts to eliminate what seem to us unnecessary steps. But we do not know the role of each experience in the total plan of God. So he often does not show us tomorrow until it becomes today.

God uses this method of dealing with us to protect us from the danger of distraction. Life is complex. We frequently cannot give our full attention to more than one day's events. Every athletic coach knows the danger of a team "looking ahead"—thinking too much about next week's opponent and failing to play today's game well. The baseball infielder who tries to throw the ball to first base before he has caught it, and the football receiver who attempts to run with the ball before he has adequately gathered in the pass, are familiar illustrations of this problem.

I have driven the interstate highway between the Minneapolis–St. Paul area and Chicago dozens of times, so many times that the car can almost make the turns automatically. Whenever I leave the Twin Cities and cross the St. Croix River into Wisconsin, I see the sign "Interstate 94" and give a sigh of relief. Gone are the stop signs, the intersections, the slowing and accelerating, the stopping and starting. There will be no stop signs or stop lights until the first toll plaza of the Illinois Tollway, some three hundred miles ahead.

Sometimes I've thought about how it would be if the instructions on the interstate were all grouped together at the beginning, with none farther. As I pulled onto 94 I'd see all the intersection signs, the markings for all the roads, and the names of the towns to which they lead. There would be a sign, "Rest stop 34 miles ahead," another "58 miles," another "89 miles." A sign would announce, "Prepare to stop, pay toll 300 miles ahead." There would be a cluster of 294 signs warning, "Keep right except to pass," and a veritable forest of 462 signs, all identically proclaiming, "No stopping except for emergencies." If highways were marked this way, it would be chaos! I would have to stop for half an hour to take notes, because from then on there would be nothing. Fortunately, highways are not marked this way. It is not necessary. Most of us have good enough brakes to stop in less than 300 miles. We think it is helpful to be warned a mile or two in advance, but that is sufficient.

Signs posted along highways give us information only as we need it and can use it. God deals with us similarly. We often do not need to understand next week's decisions today. If we had the information now, we would find it difficult to concentrate upon today's decisions and actions.

This idea of God's day-by-day leading has been well expressed in John Henry Newman's hymn:

> Lead, kindly Light, amid the encircling gloom,
> Lead thou me on;
> The night is dark, and I am far from home;
> Lead thou me on:
> Keep thou my feet; I do not ask to see
> The distant scene—one step enough for me.[1]

It is natural for us to want to guarantee the future. Being fallible and finite, we attempt to acquire enough wealth, wisdom, skill, or influence to be able to protect ourselves against the uncertainties of tomorrow. Every guarantee, however, is only as strong as what stands behind it, and human strength is limited.

Several years ago a savings and loan association in Arizona advertised its savings accounts in financial sections of newspapers across the country. The dividend rate was very favorable, and people rushed their money in. The

1. Hymn lyrics by John Henry Newman, "Lead, Kindly Light." From *Hymns for the Living Church* (Carol Stream, Ill.: Hope, 1974), p. 442.

advertisement indicated that each account was insured to $10,000. But very few people inquired about the insurance. They assumed that the accounts were insured by the Federal Savings and Loan Association, although the ad did not say that. Then difficult times came and many depositors attempted to withdraw their funds, only to find that they could not. They inquired about the insurance and were once again assured that each account was indeed insured to $10,000—by an insurance company in Morocco. Its total assets were $2,000. The guarantee was fixed, but the insurance company had no strength to deliver. Likewise, every human guarantee—because it contains an element of uncertainty—fails to effectively combat our anxiety about the future.

How much better to follow Jesus' advice: to seek first God's kingdom and his righteousness, to live by his grace and follow his commands. Then we will know that all these things will be added to us by God who, being all-powerful, controls the future and will give it to us day by day.

> Day by day and with each passing moment,
> Strength I find to meet my trials here;
> Trusting in my Father's wise bestowment,
> I've no cause for worry or for fear.
> He whose heart is kind beyond all measure
> Gives unto each day what he deems best.
> Lovingly, its part of pain and pleasure,
> Mingling toil with peace and rest.[2]

Put It into Practice

To live day by day, follow these guidelines:

1. Realize that God is not necessarily in a hurry in his working. The fact that answers to our prayers have not appeared does not mean he is not at work. It was 25 years from the time he gave the promise to Abraham and Sarah

---

2. Hymn lyrics by Carolina Sandell Berg, "Day by Day and with Each Passing Moment." From *Hymns for the Living Church*, p. 561.

DOES IT MATTER HOW I LIVE?

until Isaac was born. He allowed Israel to remain in Egypt for 430 years before he delivered them. The faithful waited for centuries for the coming of the Messiah before Jesus was born. Study and reflect upon these and similar themes of the Bible.

2. Review regularly the Scripture passages that emphasize God's provision for his creatures. Read the psalms with their testimonies of the goodness of God in the life of the believer.

3. Be careful in your expenditures, so that your future resources are not spent in advance. Be particularly cautious about entering into debt beyond major essential purchases, such as housing and transportation. Consider saving until you have enough money to pay cash for your purchases. Practice living simply, within your means. Recognize that a person's life does not consist in the abundance of possessions (Luke 12:15).

4. Be sure to do today's work with today's strength, rather than allowing responsibilities to accumulate. Be careful about taking on more than you should.

5. Look back upon God's working in your life and observe how point B has followed from point A, but that at point A you could not have anticipated point B.

6. Concentrate upon making the very best use today of all that God has revealed about today, rather than overlooking some important facet because of your curiosity about the future.

7. Notice the times in Scripture when God provided extra resources such as physical strength for a special time of need. Recognize that he will do the same in times of heavy responsibility, pain, fatigue, or sorrow.

Study Guide

Key Concept Questions

1. In what three major areas do Christians need to learn how to adjust on a "day-by-day" basis to God's ways of working?
2. Explain two probable reasons why God often arranges for our physical needs to be supplied "incrementally," that is, as we really have need of them, rather than far in advance.
3. What does the author say is the main reason why God does not reveal ahead of time what the future holds?
4. What is the one way we can be absolutely assured that God's resources will be accessible to us just when we need them?

Bible Investigation

Read the account in 1 Kings 17 of God's provision for the physical needs of the prophet Elijah and the widow of Zarephath. Then read a similar story in 2 Kings 4:1–7 of God's special provision for the prophet Elisha and another poverty-stricken widow. What principles for drawing upon God's resources can you draw from these passages? To what extent is the exercising of faith a factor in the ability to access God's day-to-day help? Precisely how was faith demonstrated by these four recipients of God's care: Elijah; the widow at Zarephath; Elisha; the dead prophet's widow?

Personal Life Application

In the fast-paced society in which we live, we may sometimes feel overwhelmed by the burden of all our responsibilities. We may even succumb to "burn-out," a condition in which our physical and emotional reserves are depleted to the extent that we may feel we don't have the strength to carry on. Reflect back upon a time when you felt particularly "depleted" or "burned out." What factors contributed to your condition? How could you have avoided this? Sometimes we "burn out" because in our self-sufficiency, we try to do it all and we end up not using our energies wisely. Read Exodus 18, and make an application for your own life based on the advice Jethro gave to his son-in-law.

For Further Thought

The author states that God deals out life one day at a time, and that therefore we should learn to live in that same day-by-day fashion. He explains that if we "seek first God's kingdom and his righteousness. . . . Then . . . all these things [daily provisions, strength, and guidance] will be added to us by God who, being all-powerful, controls the future and will give it to us day by day." Read the account in 1 Chronicles 21 describing the time that David took a census of Israel. In what ways does this incident provide a negative example of the above principle? What was the true nature of David's sin, and why was his punishment so severe and the consequences for the whole nation so disastrous? What does this account teach us about the ways in which we can actually *prevent* God from giving "unto each day what he deems best"? It is important to also observe from this example that God is able to use even our mistakes to bring about his purposes. In this case David's need for an altar (to be used to secure God's forgiveness of his sin) resulted in a positive "outcome," the purchase of the future site for the temple.

13

How to Accept Being Rejected

1 Samuel 8:1–21

Cod liver oil! I can still recall the taste of that horrible, oily, slimy substance.

For children growing up in Minnesota, the severe winters and danger of respiratory infections posed special threats to health. This was especially true for elementary school children like me, who walked a mile and a half to school each day. It was before the days of multiple vitamin capsules, so my mother followed the standard procedure for preventive medicine. On the theory that anything good for you had to taste bad, she made each of us swallow a teaspoonful of cod liver oil every morning. It should have been very beneficial.

I worked out a system to minimize the unpleasantness of the experience. I took the spoon in my right hand and a quarter slice of orange in my left hand. Then I quickly drank the oil from the spoon, took the spoon out of my mouth, bit into the orange, and sucked as hard as I could! The sweet orange juice obliterated the taste of the cod liver oil.

Life brings us many experiences of bitterness, pain, and hardship. Among the most difficult of all to endure are our experiences of rejection by other human beings, those unkind, thoughtless, or unfair acts by others in which they express disapproval of our thoughts or actions, or worse, reject us as persons.

This was the type of situation that Samuel faced. By the Lord's choosing he served as judge in Israel. He attempted, to the best of his ability, to serve well. Yet in 1 Samuel 8:1–21 we read that without warning the elders of Israel decided to depose him. They did not want him any longer; they wanted a king. How would he deal with this? More correctly, how would God deal with him through this situation? By examining Samuel's reaction we will see principles that will enable us to turn the disappointments and rejections we experience into the means of God's blessing. If we do not follow God's guidelines, our bruised feelings will eat away at our effectiveness for him.

Go to God First

The first action Samuel took was to take his pain to God. Samuel ruled over Israel just as had other judges, including Samson and Gideon before him. His position was not a hereditary or an elected one. He ruled by his personal influence and by the authority of an unseen God. He had ruled well, but now he had grown old and could no longer discharge his duties alone. He therefore appointed his sons to serve as judges with him. They had not shown any improper behavior before this time, but now they were unable to handle the power that went with the office. They accepted bribes to pervert justice.

At this point the elders of Israel came to Samuel with a twofold complaint: "You are old, and your sons do not walk in your ways" (1 Sam. 8:5). The complaint was direct and painful. No one likes to be reminded that he is growing old, or that he is not all that he once was. Further, the elders' criticism that Samuel's sons had not followed him implied that he had failed in his role as a father. Coming without warning and in such blunt form, this had to be a painful and shocking confrontation for Samuel.

These elders could have been a bit more diplomatic. Properly trained board members would probably select their most tactful member, who would take Samuel out to lunch at a nice restaurant. He would say something like, "Samuel, the council of elders has noted how long and superbly you have served as judge and we will be forever indebted to you. We know that we will never be able to find anyone who can replace you. We feel, however, that it is just not fair for us to take advantage of you in this way any longer. You have earned the right to enjoy your retirement, and we want you to enjoy those twilight years with your wife, as you have not been able to do before now because of your busy schedule and your faithful service." Then they would have thrown a big farewell party, or perhaps a whole series of them, presented him with a gold wrist-sundial, and he would have passed off the scene. That is how it should have been done. But it wasn't. "You are old, and your sons do not walk after your ways." What a stinging rebuke!

Sometimes the bitter pill will come that sharply to us, too. Tactfulness does not always mark expressions of rejection. And, like Samuel, we will find that it burns in our soul. We may be tempted to retaliate, to point out the other side of the issue, and that might well be justified in a sense.

Notice Samuel's response, however. He could have said, "You have to understand that I have done pretty well compared to the other judges you have had." He could have excused himself. Or he could have pointed out that they as a nation had likewise been far from perfect. All of this would have been true, and it might have made Samuel feel better for a time. But it would not help things in the long term. It might have led to a shouting match, merely heightening the conflict. From the scriptural account we see him give no response or rebuttal. His defense is one from silence, and it seems unlikely that anything significant would have been omitted from the written report.

Instead of responding to the elders, Samuel went to God and told him what had happened: The people had rejected him. The connection between what they had done and his prayer is clear: "But when they said, 'Give us a king to lead us,' this displeased Samuel; so he prayed to the LORD" (v. 6). His first reaction was to turn to the Lord and pour out before him his sense of pain and injustice.

That is a good practice for us to follow as well. If we seek to excuse ourselves or engage in countercriticism, we will only intensify the problem. While there are times when we should respond to unjust charges, our purpose is to avoid retaliation. Similarly, the solution to rejection is not to tell others about the wrong done to us. That spreads the problem more widely. Rather, our first reaction should be to take our verbalizations of wrong and pain to the Lord.

The Lord invites us to do this. Peter urges us: "Cast all your anxiety on him because he cares for you" (1 Pet. 5:7). Not only does God take our cares and pain, but we learn from him in the process. He teaches us what actions he wants us to take about our own shortcomings. And he directs us to the correct response Jesus prescribed for situations in which discord arises between believers (see Matt. 5:23–26).

Ask to See the Bigger Picture

A second step to tackling rejection is to grasp the larger issue involved. When Samuel brought his complaint to God, the Lord replied by saying, "Listen to all that the people are saying to you; it is not you they have rejected, but they have rejected me as their king" (1 Sam. 8:7). What Samuel thought to be the real issue was not. The truly

DOES IT MATTER HOW I LIVE?

serious problem was that the people wanted a king like other nations, instead of being ruled by an unseen God. Their desire was an offense against God. It probably was God's plan that they should eventually have a king, but this was not the time or the right reason. They wanted to be like other nations. They wanted to be a "name brand" nation. Although they had the incomparable privilege of being the chosen nation, the covenant people of the true and living God, they thought this was less valuable than the opportunity to be like every other nation.

This was a far more serious problem than Samuel had realized, because the people were actually turning away from the true and living God. They were displeasing God. And as a result they would not continue to receive his blessing. God would give them the king they were asking for, but this would result in more than they had intended. The king would exploit them and oppress them; they would cry out to God, but he would not hear them (vv. 13–18). The momentary pain that Samuel was feeling was almost nothing compared to the lasting problem that would result from this monarchy.

In view of this, the people needed to be warned, in the hope that they would turn from their foolish resolve. Instead of being unwanted and unneeded as he had felt, Samuel received an important task to carry out for Jehovah. The urgency of his task and his preoccupation with it turned Samuel's attention compellingly away from his own bruised ego.

One of the best cures for our pain and feelings of rejection is to look at the larger issues in which the Lord will involve us, if we let him. When seen in the light of God's greater eternal purposes, our temporary sense of rebuff begins to fade into insignificance. We realize that the discomfort we feel at the moment is small compared to the eternal anguish of the lost.

Another helpful thing we can do is to ask ourselves why the person who did such a seemingly harsh or cruel thing to us acted as he or she did. Frequently such actions are a sign of a very serious problem in that person's life. It is paradoxical but true that frequently the people who are the most in need of love are the ones who by their actions make themselves most difficult to love.

In many realms of experience people persevere in the face of pain because they are preoccupied with something more urgent. Soldiers have fought on in spite of serious wounds. Some athletes virtually fail to notice an injury because their whole attention is riveted upon a crucial goal. Sometimes a preacher speaking in a hot auditorium is much less affected than his less active listeners because he is caught up in what he is doing.

When we feel oppressed by a wrong done to us and bring our complaint to the Lord, he will often point out more important considerations that are at stake. We are wise to ask him to show us the larger issues when we pray about our hurt feelings.

Help the One Who Hurt You

The third step in dealing with the bitterness of life's experiences is to seek the welfare of the one who hurt you. Samuel might have had several reactions to his rebukers. He might have said, "If they want a king, they shall have one. I will warn them as the Lord has said, but then I will wash my hands of them. I won't help them find their king. They didn't want me to serve them any longer, so forget it. And when they get their king and he oppresses them, I'm really going to enjoy it. I'll tell them, 'I told you so.' They'll be sorry then that they rejected me. The Lord will avenge me." That would have been a very human reaction, wanting to return evil for evil. It would have given Samuel some selfish satisfaction, but it would also have caused him to become a smaller person.

Samuel might have responded with indifference. He might have said, "I'm through with them, as they are with me. I bear them no ill will, but neither do I continue to be concerned about their welfare." That would have been another human reaction, and in the eyes of some people a rather commendable one. It is a reaction of indifference or of tolerance. It enables the hurt to heal and precludes our hurting the offender. But Samuel didn't choose that course of action either.

Rather than seeking revenge or casting these people aside, Samuel resolved to do all that he could to help them. If they were determined to bring evil upon themselves and the nation, he at least would try to mitigate it as much as he could. He would be the Lord's agent in seeking the king they asked for. He would be the one through whom God would choose the second king, David, when the first king (Saul) disobeyed and lost fellowship with the Lord. When they did not heed the warning that he gave them, he could have taken that as another rebuff, but he did not. At his farewell he pled with them and urged them not to turn away from serving the Lord to idols (12:20–22). And then he pledged to continue to pray for them. He saw it in the context of his continued faithfulness to the Lord: "As for me, far be it from me that I should sin against the Lord by failing to pray for you" (12:23).

When someone has hurt and rejected us, we will be tempted to want to retaliate, or at least to cast him or her away. But that is not a permanent solution to our problem, and it certainly is not pleasing to God. As hard as it may seem, we need to ask the Lord to show us what we can do to help the offending person or people, and to give us the strength to do it. That is what real love is about. It is not feeling good and warm toward the other person. If that were the case, Jesus' command to "love your neighbor as yourself" would be an impossible instruction to follow, because our emotions are not under that kind of direct voluntary control. But love is concern and action for the ultimate good of the other person, regardless of how we feel toward him or her. It is an act of will rather than a matter of emotions.

Because our Lord has designed and created us, he knows that this command is not only theologically sound; it is psychologically sound, too. The best way to prevent hurt from becoming a bitterness that harms us as much or much more than the person toward whom we direct it is to seek to do good to that person.

On one occasion I was stranded in Philadelphia for twenty-six hours. O'Hare Airport in Chicago, where I wanted to go, was closed because of a snowstorm. By the second day I was becoming irritated at everyone, including the airline personnel. I had decided that perhaps the person who said, "TWA means Try Walking Across," was right. I had finished all the work I brought with me, so I went to the newsstand to find something to read. My eye snagged on a book titled *How to Get Along with Other People.* I felt I needed that book. It was not a Christian book or even a religious book. It was written from a secular psychological standpoint. As I skimmed it I found a statement that, from the consideration of one's own mental health, the best thing to do when someone else has wronged you is find the first opportunity to do something nice for him or her and do it. Secular psychology agrees with biblical truth at this point.

The point is: Samuel followed God's way, and what was best for the other party was also best for him. God's way is to return good for evil.

There are many ways that people respond to rejection and hurt. Some allow painful memories to fester in their souls, and carry the resentment to their graves. In so doing they damage the beauty that might have been present in their lives. What a loss. God's way is better.

We've all seen pearls. We think they are beautiful and valuable. And we know how they were formed. The process begins when a sharp and abrasive object, often just a grain of sand or mud, makes its way inside an oyster's shell. The oyster has all its protection on the outside. Its body is soft and vulnerable. There is only one way that it can protect itself from harm by this offending intruder. It exudes a milky substance that coats the object and makes it smooth, so that it does not cut and tear the oyster's body. As it does so, it makes the painful foreign object a thing of beauty.

That's what an oyster does with its hurts. What do you do with yours?

Put It into Practice

You can overcome the pain of being rejected by making sure that you:

1. Take your hurt and complaint first to God, who knows and understands you, rather than lash back in an attempt to hurt the other or justify and defend yourself. Go to God rather than complain to others about your offender.

2. Ask God what the important issue in all of this really is. What would he want to see done in this situation? In particular, why has this person acted in this way? What is his or her problem or need?

3. See what action you can take to help the other person and do it, not in a way that will embarrass the other, but genuinely to bring about good.

4. Continue to pray for the person.

5. Do not let go of or avoid the person.

6. Do not hope for harm to come to the other.

7. Ask God to use this experience to bring strength and maturity into your life.

Study Guide

Key Concept Questions

1. Describe some typical ways in which we are apt to respond to disapproval and rejection by others. How do these compare with the way Samuel reacted when he was rejected by the elders of Israel (1 Sam. 8:1–21)?
2. List three steps for dealing with rejection that we can derive from Samuel's experience.
3. What can be accomplished by God when we bring our complaints about others' hurtful words or actions first to him?
4. According to the author, how is Jesus' command to "love your enemies" to be concretely carried out in response to hurtful rejection?
5. Describe the benefits of dealing with hurt the way that Samuel did.

Bible Investigation

One individual who experienced continuous rejection from almost everyone around him was the prophet Jeremiah. Explore the following passages in order to discover the full extent to which Jeremiah was rejected: Jeremiah 11:18–23; 12:6; 20:1–2, 10; 26:7–11; 28:1–17; 36:20–26.

Next, read Jeremiah 12 and 20. Analyze Jeremiah's responses to rejection from these passages and compare it to that of Samuel. Would you say that Jeremiah desired to "seek the welfare" of those who rejected him? Why or why not?

Personal Life Application

Everyone experiences the pain of rejection at some point in his or her life. The way a person responds to this experience can bring either increased strength and maturity, or in contrast, a crippling kind of resentment that inhibits further growth. Reflect back upon a past incident when you felt like retaliating against someone who criticized or hurt you. What was the outcome of this hurtful experience? How did you overcome the pain of being rejected? What is your relationship with that person like today?

When we are experiencing the pain of rejection we can become tempted to defensively heap criticism upon those who hurt us. We may even vent our anger upon innocent "bystanders"! The passages below are representative of those found throughout Scripture that speak of the kind of attitude we are to maintain in our relationships with others—even in unpleasant situations. After reading the verses, evaluate your present relationships in order to become aware of ways in which you could be maintaining an unhealthy resentment, thereby reducing your own effectiveness and contributing to someone else's pain. Romans 12:3, 9–21; Galatians 5:26; Philippians 2:1–11; James 2:1–13.

Resolve today not only to "help" in some concrete way a person who has wronged you, but also to promote harmony with someone you yourself may have slighted.

For Further Thought

IDEA A

Read Peter's admonition for dealing with unjust suffering in 1 Peter 2:12, 18–23 (esp. v. 23). How should this counsel affect our response to those who reject us? Read also the account of personal rejection experienced by Jephthah the Gileadite in Judges 11:1–11. Taken together, what do these passages tell us about how God can work out his will even in unjust circumstances?

IDEA B

Does the command to "bear up under the pain of unjust suffering" (1 Pet. 2:19) mean that Christians should always submit to injustice and never stand up for their rights? Refer to the case of Zelophehad's daughters in Numbers 27.

Teaching Suggestions

Chapter 1. If the Gospel Is So Simple, Why Is Godly Living So Hard?

1. Use the question posed in this chapter's title as a "focus question" for this session. Begin by asking class members if they agree with the underlying premise implied in the question (that the gospel itself is simple, but that godly living is hard). As they share ideas, ask why this is often the case. Use the humorous story of the frustrated woodcutter as an illustration, guiding the discussion to the conclusion that although we can know a great deal about *what* we ought to do in our Christian lives, our knowledge of *how* to do what we know often escapes us. Explain that although this awareness of the disparity between our understanding and our actual performance of the Christian life can be a real source of frustration, God's grace is always sufficient for us when we really want to fulfill God's expectations of us.

2. Present from the text the three categories of believers whose performance in the Christian life falls short of the standards found in Scripture ("Key Concept Question" #3). Ask class members to choose the category with which they can most easily identify. Point out that the objec-

tive of this study will be to help them become better followers of Christ by learning how to use God's own resources to do what he expects them to do.

3. Proceed through the "Bible Investigation" section to help class members relate to a biblical personality who "struggled" in the same ways we do today, but who through his or her struggle learned how to please God.

4. Continue in Bible study by following the instructions provided in the "For Further Thought" section. Point out that living by the Spirit will manifest itself with the "fruit" of the Spirit (Gal. 5:16–26), and that all of these are demonstrated in the context of relationships.

5. Conclude this session with the "Personal Life Application" section. Depending on the composition of the group, you may choose to do this individually and privately, or as a group activity (sharing together the "struggles" that can be prayed for corporately). Close by expressing gratitude to God for his grace, which enables us to do everything through him who gives strength.

Provide class members with a calendar listing topics to be discussed each week.

Chapter 2. When You Absolutely, Positively Have to Know You're Saved

1. To begin this session, read aloud the author's description of his own agonizing boyhood struggle with doubt concerning the certainty of his salvation. Ask volunteers to share what their conversion stories were like. To what degree did emotions play a part in these experiences?

2. Following the instructions provided in the "Bible Investigation" section, read through Romans 8 for the purpose of finding verses providing assurance of salvation. As group members discover important truths, first write them down on chart paper, then try to group them according to their common elements. The goal is to arrive at the three "sources" of assurance described by the

author: the Word of God, the works of the Christian life, and the witness of the Spirit.

3. Present the four specific ways in which one's life will give evidence of the reality of the work God has done for each believer. Then use Idea A from the "For Further Thought" section as a springboard for discussion. Include the illustration about Willie Horton to help class members focus on "how far they have come" rather than "how far they must yet go" when attempting to evaluate the presence of "works" in the Christian life.

4. Turn to the passages suggested in Idea B of the "For Further Thought" section in order to come to an understanding of what is meant by the "witness of the Spirit." Emphasize that the Spirit's witness does not occur apart from the Word of God, and therefore will never contradict it.

5. Consider together the implications of knowing for sure that you are saved. What results can come from such confident living? For believer themselves? For the kingdom of God?

6. If there is time, follow the directions provided in the "Personal Life Application" section. You may wish to do this activity in small groups and then share results.

7. In order to further underscore the assurance of salvation found in God's Word, ask class members to share their favorite verses or passages of assurance and promise. Spend time in prayer thanking God for the assurance that he has provided.

Chapter 3. Getting to Know Your Best Friend Better

1. Write the following focus question on the board: "How would you describe the nature of Jesus' relationship to his followers?" (You will refer to this question later.)

2. Begin this session by asking class members to reflect upon one of their most rewarding and enduring friend-

ships. Identify some of the characteristics of these special relationships. Refer now to the focus question. Elicit some initial responses; then use the following "I am" passages from the Book of John to examine how Jesus described his relationship to others: 6:35; 8:12; 10:9; 10:14; 14:6; 15:5; 15:15; 18:37. From these verses, which analogy or image of the relationship between Jesus and his followers do you find the most attractive? Why?

3. Use the "Bible Investigation" section to focus on the special qualities of the enduring friendship between David and Jonathan. Draw parallels between these qualities and the characteristics of friendship with Jesus found in John 15:9–17.

4. Ask class members to consider those things that can prevent a friendship from deepening. (List these on the board.) Then ask how a friendship relationship with Jesus can be disrupted. (Point out how disobedience can sever one's relationship with Jesus.) What should be our attitude toward obedience to Jesus' commands? Describe from the text the two erroneous extremes in understanding our motivation to please God.

5. Conclude this session with the concepts presented in the "For Further Thought" section. Point out that friendship with God requires the willingness to bring Jesus' message and extend his compassion to the lost and needy in this world while at the same time not succumbing to the world's standards. To be friends with Jesus can result in persecution by the world, yet our friend Jesus assures us, "In this world you will have trouble. But take heart! I have overcome the world" (John 16:33).

Chapter 4. How to Find Success in Your Prayer Life

1. Write the following focus question on the board: "If it is true that God is omniscient and therefore knows all about our needs, and if it is also true that he is totally sovereign and is therefore certain to work out his will in

heaven and in earth, then why do we need to pray? What really does prayer accomplish?"

To help answer this question, first read through (as a group) the passage illustrated in Luke 11:1–13. Discuss together what we learn about the conditions for effective prayer from this passage ("Key Concept Question" #1).

2. Proceed through the instructions in the "Personal Life Application" section, pointing out how improper motives and worldly preoccupations can prevent us from using prayer to link up with God's purposes.

3. Reinforce the understanding of the requirements for effective prayer by thoughtfully examining the passages found in both the "Bible Investigation" and "For Further Thought—Idea A" sections. Point out that when Asa failed to follow God's plan, it became impossible for him even to pray, let alone be effective in prayer.

4. Conclude this session by discussing any "Key Concept Questions" not yet addressed. If there is time, consider the problem raised by those who would say that Christians should "name it and claim it" (Idea B in the "For Further Thought" section). Emphasize the fact that so often what is "named" in hopes of being "claimed" by these Christians arises from selfish wants that do not in any way connect with what God wants to have happen in his world.

Chapter 5. Resisting Temptation Without Backing Down

1. Write the following focus question on the board: "If you have made a decision to follow Christ, and the Holy Spirit has come to dwell within you, then how is it that temptation can still be a problem?" (Save discussion of this question until later in this session.)

2. Read together Matthew 4:1–11, which describes Jesus' experience of temptation. Outline the four essentials for resisting temptation from the text. As part of this pre-

sentation, include the "subpoint" material that will help class members answer "Key Concept Questions" 1–4.

3. Follow the instructions in the "Bible Investigation" section, pointing out similarities and differences in the responses to temptation between Adam and Eve and Joseph. Underscore the point that although Adam and Eve did not have the benefit of as much "progressive" revelation as Joseph (passed on from Abraham, Isaac, and Jacob), they had the benefit of having received God's explicit warning, including knowledge of the direct consequences of disobedience.

4. Continue the discussion of the nature of temptation by asking the questions provided in the two "For Further Thought" sections. Refer to the Scripture references in order to formulate responses. Note (Idea A) that the essence of sin is a prideful self-sufficiency that refuses to acknowledge God as God. Sin finds its expression in disobedience to the moral law of God. Satan is continually motivated to tempt believers in order to shift their allegiance away from God. Note also (Idea B) that God does not lead individuals into temptation. He does, however, permit Satan to tempt people to sin, but it is always the individual who actually makes the decision to *act* on the temptation.

5. Use the example of Samson from the "Personal Life Application" section to explain how Satan is always at work at our "weak spots," not only when we are the "weakest," but also when we appear "strong." Times of apparent strength can in reality be times when Satan is successful in leading us to depend upon our own power— apart from dependence upon God.

6. Conclude this session by referring back to the focus question in step 1. After some initial discussion, refer to Galatians 5:13–6:10. Emphasize that sin is a persistent problem because of the conflicting forces within each of us. Although the Holy Spirit is infinitely more powerful than the sinful nature, we, by our own evil

desires and wrong choices, can override the promptings of the Holy Spirit. Yet by drawing upon the resources that God has provided—by understanding the factors at work in temptation and by acting upon this knowledge—we can successfully "resist temptation without backing down!"

Chapter 6. The Hidden Value of Doubt

1. Write the following focus question on the board, but do not attempt to answer it until the end of the session: "In the life of a Christian, is doubt a positive or a negative?"

Introduce the discussion by defining doubt, highlighting the author's distinction between doubt and disbelief or unbelief. Then ask a volunteer to read aloud the focus passage (Luke 7:18–30).

Discuss together the way that Jesus responded to John's expression of doubt.

2. Follow the instructions in the "Bible Investigation" section, assigning the various Bible characters to small groups to research and then report their findings to the group. Summarize by pointing out the patience that God demonstrated toward those expressing honest doubt. Perhaps God showed less patience in the case of Zechariah because he was a priest performing a priestly function; thus Zechariah's questioning of God's promise was presumptuous.

3. Discuss together the instances when doubt is likely to become a problem. Present the author's argument that our need for certainty is in direct proportion to the seriousness of our commitment to something—to what we have risked upon its truth. Include those times in which hardships and suffering can trigger doubt.

4. At this point use the "Personal Life Application" section to determine together steps you can take to get in control of doubt. Point out how the application of wisdom, prayer, and trusting in God can help dispel doubt.

Include in this discussion the other "Put It into Practice" steps that the author provides at the end of the chapter.

5. Conclude this session by emphasizing the "voluntary" nature of doubt (see the "For Further Thought" section). Flesh out this idea with the author's assertion that we are able to choose what we will focus our attention on, and that therefore we can help to dispel doubt by looking carefully at the evidence that God gives us.

Answer the focus question by explaining that the "hidden value" of doubt is that it can give rise to the occasion to learn that "right response" and thereby to reconnect with those plans of God that "go on for ever and ever."

Chapter 7. How to Know You Know God's Will

1. Write the following focus question on the board: "When making important decisions about my life, how can I determine God's will in the matter?" Brainstorm together some initial responses, then use textual material to identify the four "channels" of God's guidance. Continue the discussion by referring to the text to answer all three "Key Concept Questions."

2. Proceed through the "Bible Investigation," "Personal Life Application," and "For Further Thought" sections in the order that they appear, taking note of the following emphases:

a. You may wish to refer to other verses that give examples of the application of wisdom (the ability to appropriately apply scriptural principles) to learning God's will. Examples are 1 Thessalonians 3:1–2; Philippians 2:25–26; Acts 6:2–6; 15:5–22.

b. You may wish to share the following humorous story to embellish the discussion about trying to determine God's will through the interpretation of circumstances:

Perhaps you have heard the story about the young farmer who wanted to know God's will for his life. Each day before he went out to work in the field, he would pray, and actually *beg* God to reveal His will to him. What should he do with his life? Then one day as he was toiling away, the clouds near the horizon seemed to come together in an unmistakable combination of letters: "PP—C," "'P— 'C", 'P'—'C'," the young farmer pondered over and over. "What could 'P'—'C' possibly mean?" Then it hit him! "PREACH CHRIST!" Finally he knew. He was to become a preacher and preach Christ! He rushed to his pastor's home and told him the great news, and asked if he might have the privilege of preaching his first sermon the next Sunday. The pastor was reluctant, but agreed. After the sermon the following Sunday, the young farmer met the pastor in his study and asked, "Well, what do you think?" The pastor replied, "Son, I'm not sure if the Lord was speaking to you in the clouds the other day or not, but if he was, I think He was telling you to *plant corn!*"

3. Close this session by referring back to the focus question. How would the initial responses of the group now be modified to reflect new learning from this lesson?

Chapter 8. How to Be Confident You're Doing God's Will

1. Begin this session by asking class members to jot down a definition of "faith." After some ideas are shared, refer to Hebrews 10:35–39 and ask, "What insights does this passage give us for providing an understanding of what it means to actually *'live* in faith'?"

2. If someone from the class recited Hebrews 11:1 as his or her "definition of faith" in step 1 above, you will have a natural transition to the "Bible Investigation" section. Point out that perhaps it is more accurate to say that this verse provides more of a description of the *outcome* of faith, rather than a complete definition of faith. A more

comprehensive definition could be discovered by looking at chapter 11 in its entirety. Now use the material provided in the "Bible Investigation" section to lead to the conclusion that the element of obedience is essential to a proper understanding of faith. Faith is not simply an intellectual assent to knowledge of the gospel, or a "blind optimism," or a "hope for" attitude, or "believing hard" that something you want to happen will eventually happen. Faith carries with it the performance of its demands. Rahab, Barak, and Jephthah were commended because at some point in their lives, they responded to God in faith by *acting* upon what they knew to be true from him.

3. Refer to the situation and questions posed in the "Personal Life Application" section. Using the two passages in Romans and James, draw out the conclusion that in order to accomplish God's will, careful thinking and wise planning are important, but we should be sure to hold all plans somewhat "loosely," always humbly submitting them before God. It is important to note that when obstacles arise that confound a "sound" plan, it should *not* necessarily be abandoned; it may simply mean that God is adjusting the timing!

4. There are times when being confident of doing God's will is not so easy. This is especially true when trying to make decisions pertaining to tough moral dilemmas like abortion, homosexuality, euthanasia, and the use of nuclear weapons. Consider the dilemmas faced by the Hebrew midwives and by Rahab. Brainstorm some guidelines to use to help resolve situations in which two biblical absolutes seem to collide.

Chapter 9. Giving to God— Many Happy Returns?

1. Place the following focus question on the board: "Do you believe that the practice of tithing (giving one-tenth of your income to the Lord) is applicable for Christians today?" Allow for a few responses before directing the

DOES IT MATTER HOW I LIVE?

group to the "For Further Thought" section. Use the textual material to present and support the author's proposition that God expects Christians today to obey the command to tithe. Point out that "tithers" today would apply all New Testament principles that suggest "proportionate giving" to gifts that exceed the tithe.

Next, outline the principles for giving found in 2 Corinthians 8–9. These are important principles to govern the practice of giving, whether they are applied to giving that replaces the tithe or to giving that is in addition to the tithe.

2. Discuss together "Key Concept Question" #2: "What is the nature of the primary blessing that Christians can expect when they are faithful in their giving?" Use 2 Corinthians 9:10–14 to give support for this answer. Stress the fact that "God has never promised to make all of his children wealthy." (See also Phil. 4:11–13.)

3. Combine "Key Concept Question" #3 with the "Bible Investigation" section. Emphasize the point that we cannot attempt to "buy God's favor" with obedience in giving without submitting to him in all other areas of our lives. (See also Isa. 1:10–20.) God will not grant a blessing to a sinful and rebellious people, just because they "bring in the whole tithe into the storehouse"!

4. Allow opportunity for the sharing of any personal anecdotes that have given class members insights into God's teachings in the area of tithing or other giving, and God's response to it.

5. Close this session by listening to a taped recording of Scott Wesley Brown's "Blessed to Be a Blessing." Discuss the message of this song and how it relates to the what Malachi teaches us about what God expects of his people.

Chapter 10. How to Share Your Faith— Without the Butterflies

1. Begin this session with the focus question posed by "Key Concept Question" #1. After some initial discus-

sion, use the biblical illustration (the Samaritan woman at the well) and material from the text to outline the three essentials for effective personal evangelism that the author identifies.

2. Next, use the "Bible Investigation" section to highlight the priority that God places on the work of evangelism. Draw the conclusion that because finding the lost was Jesus' primary mission on earth, and since he has now entrusted that mission to all believers, the job of proclaiming the message of reconciliation should be *our* first priority as well.

3. Brainstorm together reasons why Christians are hindered in their witness. Emphasize the extent to which simple "inertia" prevents witnessing from taking place.

4. Use the following learning activity to reinforce the skills required to be "alert," "aware," and "able to apply." Have class members write, either individually or in groups of two to three persons, a short real-life scenario in which a non-Christian spontaneously raises an issue that presents an "opening" for a Christian to share his or her faith. Exchange "scenarios" among the groups, and "rehearse" a response that would reveal to the inquirer how faith in Christ can make a difference in one's life. (If time is short, you can use the scenario provided in the "Personal Life Application" section).

5. Discuss together the ideas presented in the "For Further Thought" section. Point out that the work of evangelism is just that—work! You can expect to encounter opposition and ridicule, and consequently you will at times feel fearful and inadequate. Yet realizing that God has chosen to make his appeal to the world through us, we must remain aggressively and resolutely committed to the task! It helps to remember two other important facts: (1) we will not be without the resources we need (Acts 1:8); and (2) God will produce the results if we are faithful (1 Cor. 3:5–7).

DOES IT MATTER HOW I LIVE?

6. Conclude by asking, "Is the possibility of sharing your faith—*with* the butterflies—worth the risk?" Answer this question by listening to the lyrics of Ray Boltz's song, "Thank You."

Chapter 11. God's Cure for Discouraged Hearts

1. Begin this session by writing the following focus question on the board: "Is discouragement always a bad thing for a Christian?" After sharing some initial responses, point out that sometimes discouragement performs a useful function in that it can lead a person to discover and remedy the problem that is its cause. Emphasize the fact that Christians are just as prone to discouragement as non-Christians, but that they alone have access to God's special resources for successfully working through these difficult times.

2. Brainstorm together the causes for discouragement, first drawing from the experiences of the group, and then using the biblical account of Elijah's experience in 1 Kings 18–19 ("Bible Investigation Section"—Idea A). Next, list the three causes for discouragement discussed in the text, and together decide which of these best fits Elijah's situation.

3. Now contrast Elijah's experience with that of Nehemiah. (Follow the instructions in the "Bible Investigation Section"—Idea B). Outline the three steps that the author suggests for drawing upon God's provisions to overcome discouragement, and identify all of the ways in which Nehemiah actually followed these steps.

4. Consider the author's suggestion to "develop a God-based optimism." Use the material provided in the "Personal Life Application" section to enlarge upon this concept. Point out that individuals are always free to choose their responses to what happens to them in life, and that therefore they actually have the freedom to prevent the discouraging words and actions of others to negatively affect their moods.

5. Use the "For Further Thought" section to point out that to "depend upon God" does not mean that we have to be passively resigned to depressing circumstances that we could work to change. Healthy assertiveness that is done in love and with respect for others is compatible with a Christ-like spirit, and can free us from discouraging helplessness. Remember, Jesus himself was a very assertive individual! He knew just when and how to stand up against hypocrisy and injustice. His assertiveness was actually a result of his resolute obedience to God's command—an obedience that demonstrated the authenticity of his total trust on God.

6. Close this session by prayerfully reading together Psalms 42 and 43.

Chapter 12. How to Live on Daily Rations, and Enjoy It

1. Begin this session by posing the following discussion questions: How many times have you wished that you could know the future—perhaps even just a small "slice" of it? If you could choose to be given this ability, would you really want it? Why or why not?

After some initial discussion, describe from the text the reason why God does not show us tomorrow until it becomes today. Draw the conclusion that God does not desire for us to become anxious about events over which we have no personal control, but rather he desires that we trust in and depend upon his goodness to us on a day-by-day basis.

2. Follow the directions in the "Bible Investigation" section. Point out that at times God gives help in some very unexpected ways, and that therefore we should never give up hope no matter how desperate our situation seems. The one "ingredient" that is required for God to be able to act in our behalf, however, is a faith that exhibits itself in obedience to God's known will.

3. Use the "For Further Thought" section to further illustrate the above principle. Point out that God sees human self-sufficiency as a particularly "irksome" sin. Consequently, God's day-to-day way of providing for our needs actually serves to protect us from this kind of sinful independence apart from him. Note also from this passage how sin often affects "innocent" people alongside the "guilty." The consequences of sin seriously disrupt our relationship with God, severing the day-to-day provision that he so lovingly desires to grant to us.

4. Use the "Personal Life Application" section as a springboard for sharing among the group those times when self-sufficiency has become a temptation and a problem.

5. Close this session by reading together Psalm 18, one of David's psalms of gratitude for the protection and strength God was faithful in giving him over the years, just when he needed it!

Chapter 13. How to Accept Being Rejected

1. Write the following focus question on the board: How do you respond when you feel ignored, slighted, or rejected? Ask the question somewhat rhetorically, accepting any responses that are given.

2. Read 1 Samuel 8:1–21, which describes Samuel's experience with rejection. Present the three steps for dealing with rejection that the author identifies.

3. Use the "Bible Investigation" section to reinforce the steps described above. Point out that although Jeremiah expressed to God a desire for revenge against those who ignored and mistreated him, he acknowledged that it was the Lord himself who would settle the score. Jeremiah ultimately did seek the welfare of those who rejected him by faithfully proclaiming God's warnings to repent in spite of the persecution he suffered.

4. Discuss together the ideas in the "For Further Thought" section. Point out that God can always work out his will even when we can only see the unfairness of

a given situation. Also point out that Christians should work to correct unjust situations when possible, but that in doing so, *the goal should be to avoid retaliation.*

5. Use the Scripture references in the "Personal Life Application" section to identify the kind of attitude that is essential to maintain in all our relationships, but especially with those who have disappointed us.

Read Habakkuk 3. The prayer of Habakkuk is a reminder that God controls what happens, that he will correct injustice in his own way and in his own timing. Meanwhile we are to depend upon his strength in order to triumph over our present circumstances.